National Parliaments

Australia • Canada • China • Finland • France • Germany
Japan • Mexico • South Korea • Sweden
United Kingdom

January 2016

The Law Library of Congress, Global Legal Research Center
(202) 707-6462 (phone) • (866) 550-0442 (fax) • law@loc.gov • http://www.law.gov

Contents

Australia

Kelly Buchanan
Chief, Foreign, Comparative, and
International Law Division I

SUMMARY   Australia's federal Parliament, established in 1901, consists of two houses: the House of Representatives and the Senate. Members and senators are elected under different preferential or ranked voting systems. Senators are elected for a six-year term, with half of the Senate elected every three years, and the House of Representatives sits for a maximum of three years.

Australia is characterized as a constitutional monarchy, with the British monarch, represented by the Governor-General, as the head of state. The parliamentary system of government is largely based on the Westminster system of the United Kingdom, while the federal system, including the role and composition of the Senate, was influenced by that in place in the United States.

The legislative powers of the Parliament are set out in the Australian Constitution, which also provides for the roles of the Speaker of the House of Representatives and the President of the Senate. The legislative process includes debates and voting over three main stages in the House and a similar process in the Senate. Both houses operate committee systems to examine bills in detail and inquire into other policy matters or government administration.

I. Background

A. Establishment of the Federal Parliament

The federal Parliament of Australia was established in 1901, following the passage, by the British Parliament, of the Commonwealth of Australia Constitution Act 1900.[1] Prior to the enactment of the Constitution, the country that is now Australia was a collection of six separate, self-governing British colonies, each with their own constitution, parliament, and laws.[2] The colonies held referendums on the draft Constitution between 1898 and 1900. The Constitution came into effect on January 1, 1901, at which point the colonies becoming states in the federation called the Commonwealth of Australia. The Parliament first convened on May 9, 1901.

---

[1] Commonwealth of Australia Constitution Act 1900 (9 July 1900) (U.K.) (original), http://www.legislation.gov.uk/ukpga/1900/12/pdfs/ukpga_19000012_en.pdf, *archived at* http://perma.cc/35JL-HHAM; Commonwealth of Australia Constitution Act 1900 (Cth) (current) (Australian Constitution), https://www.comlaw.gov.au/Details/C2013Q00005, *archived at* http://perma.cc/CF8R-SERL.

[2] *The Colonial Parliaments of Australia*, PARLIAMENTARY EDUCATION OFFICE, http://www.peo.gov.au/learning/closer-look/short-history/the-colonial-parliaments-of-australia.html (last visited Nov. 27, 2015), *archived at* http://perma.cc/TJ6G-N4AX.

In addition to the six founding states, the Commonwealth of Australia now includes three self-governing territories; two on the mainland (Northern Territory and Australian Capital Territory (ACT)) and one external (Norfolk Island). Seven other external territories are non-self-governing.[3]

B. Location of the Parliament

Between 1901 and 1927, the Commonwealth Parliament met in the Victorian Parliament House in Melbourne. This was not intended to be the permanent location of the Parliament; in fact, the Constitution stated that the seat of federal government should be in New South Wales, within 100 miles of Sydney. In 1908, the Parliament voted for a new federal capital to be established at Canberra,[4] which was then located in southern New South Wales but is now in the ACT. The Provisional Parliament House (now known as Old Parliament House) was opened in Canberra in 1927, with Parliament sitting in that building until 1988, when it moved to a permanent building on Capital Hill.[5]

Canberra is a planned city. There was an international contest to design the capital city, which was won by two architects from Chicago. Construction of the city commenced in 1913.[6]

The design of the current Parliament House is based on the shape of two boomerangs. There is a large flag pole on the top of the building. The building contains 4,700 rooms. The Senate chamber is decorated in red, while the House chamber is decorated in green. The building contains a Ministerial Wing, which houses the offices of the prime minister and other ministers.[7]

---

[3] *State and Territory Government*, AUSTRALIAN GOVERNMENT, http://www.australia.gov.au/about-government/how-government-works/state-and-territory-government (last visited Nov. 30, 2015), *archived at* http://perma.cc/US57-3KAQ.

[4] *History of the Capital*, NATIONAL CAPITAL AUTHORITY, https://www.nationalcapital.gov.au/index.php/education/history-of-the-capital (last updated Jan. 12, 2015), *archived at* https://perma.cc/6NH6-HJYF.

[5] PARLIAMENTARY EDUCATION OFFICE, A SHORT HISTORY OF PARLIAMENT 10, http://www.peo.gov.au/uploads/peo/docs/closer-look/CloserLook_Short-History-of-Parliament.pdf (last visited Nov. 27, 2015), *archived at* http://perma.cc/2HMY-T796.

[6] *Canberra – Australia's Capital City*, AUSTRALIAN GOVERNMENT, http://www.australia.gov.au/about-australia/australian-story/canberra-australias-capital-city (last updated Sept. 14, 2015), *archived at* http://perma.cc/658C-3ZAM.

[7] *Architecture and Architect*, PARLIAMENT OF AUSTRALIA, http://www.aph.gov.au/Visit_Parliament/About_the_Building/Architecture_and_the_Architect (last visited Nov. 27, 2015), *archived at* http://perma.cc/BPC5-Y3PE; *Parliament House*, PARLIAMENTARY EDUCATION OFFICE, http://www.peo.gov.au/learning/fact-sheets/parliament-house.html (last visited Nov. 27, 2015), *archived at* http://perma.cc/7HNZ-PQM5.

II. Constitutional Status and Role

A. Australian System of Government

Australia is characterized as being "a constitutional monarchy, a parliamentary democracy and a federation."[8] The Constitution established Australia as a constitutional monarchy, with the head of state being the British monarch ("the Queen"[9]), represented in Australia by the Governor-General of the Commonwealth of Australia.[10] The parliamentary system of government in Australia is based on the Westminster system of the United Kingdom, while the federal system was influenced by the model established under the Constitution of the United States.[11]

Under the parliamentary system, members of the federal executive, including the Prime Minister, who is the head of the executive branch of government, are drawn from those elected to the Parliament. In essence, "the party or coalition of parties which commands the support of a majority in the House assumes the Government and the largest minority party (or coalition of parties) the Opposition."[12] The Prime Minister is the leader of the majority party or coalition, as selected by that group, and is commissioned by the Governor-General.

Both members and senators can be appointed as "Ministers of State" by the Governor-General on the advice of the Prime Minister;[13] in fact, "in recent decades senators have usually comprised approximately one quarter to one third of the ministry."[14] The full group of ministers ("the ministry"), or a select group of ministers, "becomes the principal policy and decision-making group of government which is commonly known as the Cabinet."[15] The decisions of Cabinet are given legal effect upon their formal ratification by the Federal Executive Council, which

---

[8] HOUSE OF REPRESENTATIVES PRACTICE, ch. 1 ("Composition") (6th ed., Sept. 2012), http://www.aph.gov.au/About_Parliament/House_of_Representatives/Powers_practice_and_procedure/Practice6/Practice6HTML, *archived at* http://perma.cc/6QC7-U7PK.

[9] This originally referred to Queen Victoria, with Covering Clause 2 of the Commonwealth of Australia Constitution Act extending the provisions of the Constitution to her successors.

[10] Australian Constitution s 2. The Governor-General is appointed by the Queen on the advice of the Prime Minister.

[11] *Senate Brief No. 9 – Origins of the Senate*, PARLIAMENT OF AUSTRALIA (Sept. 2015), http://www.aph.gov.au/About_Parliament/Senate/Powers_practice_n_procedures/Senate_Briefs/Brief09, *archived at* http://perma.cc/T4HH-UKFR.

[12] HOUSE OF REPRESENTATIVES PRACTICE, *supra* note 8, ch. 1 ("Functions of the House").

[13] Australian Constitution, s 64.

[14] *Senate Brief No. 14 – Ministers in the Senate*, PARLIAMENT OF AUSTRALIA (Sept. 2015), http://www.aph.gov.au/About_Parliament/Senate/Powers_practice_n_procedures/Senate_Briefs/Brief14, *archived at* http://perma.cc/Y6TJ-JW5D.

[15] HOUSE OF REPRESENTATIVES PRACTICE, *supra* note 8, ch. 2 ("Government and Parliament Relationships").

comprises all ministers with the Governor-General presiding.[16] The Governor-General acts on the advice of the ministry "on virtually all matters."[17]

The Prime Minister and the rest of the ministry are accountable to the Parliament through various mechanisms.[18] Under the Westminster-based system, the "Opposition" has "the officially recognized function, established by convention, of opposing the Government."[19] In addition to having equal time for expressing views on legislation and other matters initiated by the government, members of the opposition (and other nongovernment members of the House and Senate) are able to question ministers directly during "question time," as well as by submitting written questions for written response.[20] Question time takes place at 2:00 p.m. each sitting day in both houses, with individual ministers being questioned, mostly without notice, on matters for which they are responsible.

B. Legislative Role of the Parliament Under the Constitution

Section 1 of the Constitution states that the legislative power of the Commonwealth is vested in three components: the Queen, the Senate, and the House of Representatives.[21] Subject to the Constitution, the Parliament is empowered to make laws for the "peace, order, and good governance of the Commonwealth."[22] The principle legislative powers of the Parliament are set out in sections 51 and 52 of the Constitution. However, "the legislative powers of these sections cannot be regarded in isolation as other constitutional provisions extend, limit, restrict or qualify their provisions."[23]

Section 52 determines areas within the exclusive jurisdiction of the Parliament, including the seat of government of the Commonwealth, matters relating to any Commonwealth government

---

[16] *Parliament and Government*, PARLIAMENT OF AUSTRALIA, http://www.aph.gov.au/About_Parliament/Work_of_the_Parliament/Forming_and_Governing_a_Nation/parl (last visited Nov. 27, 2015), *archived at* http://perma.cc/JZE9-EAW8.

[17] *Id.*

[18] *House of Representatives Infosheet 1 – Questions*, PARLIAMENT OF AUSTRALIA (Feb. 2014), http://www.aph.gov.au/About_Parliament/House_of_Representatives/Powers_practice_and_procedure/00_-_Infosheets/Infosheet_1_-_Questions (last visited Nov. 27, 2015), *archived at* http://perma.cc/4VWQ-HKRJ.

[19] *House of Representatives Infosheet 19 – Government and Opposition*, PARLIAMENT OF AUSTRALIA (Feb. 2014), http://www.aph.gov.au/About_Parliament/House_of_Representatives/Powers_practice_and_procedure/00_-_Infosheets/Infosheet_19_-_The_House_-_Government_and_Opposition (last visited Nov. 27, 2015), *archived at* http://perma.cc/4WVN-NBWR.

[20] *House of Representatives Infosheet 1 – Questions, supra* note 18; *Senate Brief No. 12 – Questions*, PARLIAMENT OF AUSTRALIA (Sept. 2015), http://www.aph.gov.au/About_Parliament/Senate/Powers_practice_n_procedures/Senate_Briefs/Brief12, *archived at* http://perma.cc/5KYH-6VAS. *See also* ODGERS' AUSTRALIAN SENATE PRACTICE, ch. 19 (13th ed., May 2012), http://www.aph.gov.au/About_Parliament/Senate/Powers_practice_n_procedures/odgers13, *archived at* http://perma.cc/JCU8-NSFM.

[21] Australian Constitution s 2.

[22] *Id.* s 51.

[23] HOUSE OF REPRESENTATIVES PRACTICE, *supra* note 8, ch. 1 ("Powers and Jurisdiction of the Houses").

department, and other matters declared by the Constitution.[24] Section 51 sets out 39 "heads of power" under which the Parliament can make laws. Some of these itemized powers may be regarded as exclusive to the Commonwealth Parliament and some are concurrently exercised with state legislatures. Areas not specified in this section are regarded as remaining within the jurisdiction of the states and are known as "residual powers."[25] Where a state legislates in an area for which the federal Parliament has concurrent powers, such legislation is subject to section 109 of the Constitution, which states that in the case of any inconsistency between a state law and Commonwealth law, the Commonwealth law shall prevail to the extent of the inconsistency.[26]

Matters on which the federal Parliament can make laws include "international and interstate trade; foreign affairs; defence; immigration; taxation; banking; insurance; marriage and divorce; currency and weights and measures; post and telecommunications; and invalid and old age pensions." [27] However, the Commonwealth has "increasingly extended its legislative competence" through its use of section 96 of the Constitution, which relates to financial assistance to the states. [28] Examples of this are seen in areas such as health, education, and transport.

The Australian Constitution provides the Senate with virtually the same power to legislate as the House of Representatives. However, the House has greater legislative powers than the Senate with regard to "the collection and expenditure of public money."[29] Appropriation and taxation bills cannot originate in the Senate, and the Senate cannot amend taxation bills and some types of appropriations bills, although it can ask the House to make amendments.

III. Structure and Composition

A. House and Senate Membership

Today, the House of Representatives is comprised of 150 members, with each member representing an electoral division.[30] Each House is elected for a period of up to three years.

Similar to the federal system in the United States, the Constitution requires that each state has an equal number of senators, being no less than six, regardless of the population of the different

---

[24] Australian Constitution s 52.

[25] HOUSE OF REPRESENTATIVES PRACTICE, *supra* note 8, ch. 1 ("Powers and Jurisdiction of the Houses").

[26] Australian Constitution s 109.

[27] *House of Representatives Infosheet 7 – Making Laws*, PARLIAMENT OF AUSTRALIA (Aug. 2014), http://www.aph.gov.au/About_Parliament/House_of_Representatives/Powers_practice_and_procedure/00_-_Infosheets/Infosheet_7_-_Making_laws (last visited Nov. 27, 2015), *archived at* http://perma.cc/HT9K-SCSZ.

[28] HOUSE OF REPRESENTATIVES PRACTICE, *supra* note 8, ch. 1 ("Powers and Jurisdiction of the Houses").

[29] *House of Representatives Infosheet 7 – Making Laws*, *supra* note 27.

[30] *About the House of Representatives*, PARLIAMENT OF AUSTRALIA, http://www.aph.gov.au/About_Parliament/House_of_Representatives/About_the_House_of_Representatives (last visited Nov. 27, 2015), *archived at* http://perma.cc/6U57-V6LB.

states.[31] There are currently 76 senators: twelve for each of the six states, along with two each from ACT and Northern Territory. State senators are elected for a term of six years, with a rotation system ensuring that half the Senate retires every three years. The four senators from the two territories are elected every three years.[32]

The two houses of Parliament are elected under different voting systems, as discussed in Part IV, below.

B. Political Parties

There are currently three main political parties represented in the House of Representatives: the Australian Labor Party, the Liberal Party of Australia, and the Nationals (previously called the National Party of Australia).[33] There are four other smaller parties with representatives in the current House as well as two independent members.[34]

At various times since 1949, there have been official coalition agreements between the parties now called the Liberal Party of Australia and the Nationals, as well as other state-level center-right parties.[35] The center-right Liberal-Nationals Coalition (the Coalition) gained a majority of the seats in the House of Representatives in the 2013 federal election and is therefore currently running a coalition government. As the major nongoverning party in the House, the center-left Australian Labor Party currently forms the official Opposition.

The division of seats in the House of Representatives as at October 2015 is as follows:[36]

- Coalition: 90 (Liberal Party of Australia, 74; Nationals, 15; Country Liberal Party, 1)
- Australian Labor Party: 55
- Australian Greens: 1
- Katter's Australian Party: 1
- Palmer United Party: 1
- Independents: 2

---

[31] Australian Constitution, s 7.

[32] *About the Senate*, PARLIAMENT OF AUSTRALIA, http://www.aph.gov.au/About_Parliament/Senate/About_the_Senate (last visited Nov. 27, 2015), *archived at* http://perma.cc/NB74-5CUS.

[33] *House of Representatives Infosheet 22 – Political Parties*, PARLIAMENT OF AUSTRALIA (Jan. 2014), http://www.aph.gov.au/About_Parliament/House_of_Representatives/Powers_practice_and_procedure/00_-_Infosheets/Infosheet_22_-_Political_parties, *archived at* http://perma.cc/4XRQ-F3KY.

[34] *See Members*, PARLIAMENT OF AUSTRALIA, http://www.aph.gov.au/Senators_and_Members/Members (last visited Nov. 27, 2015), *archived at* http://perma.cc/N27U-8XS6.

[35] *House of Representatives Infosheet 22 – Political Parties*, *supra* note 33.

[36] *Statistics for the 44th Parliament*, PARLIAMENTARY EDUCATION OFFICE, http://www.peo.gov.au/learning/parliament-now/statistics.html (statistics as of Oct. 22, 2015), *archived at* http://perma.cc/2GPU-TBTM.

The party composition of the Senate is as follows:

- Coalition: 33 (Liberal Party of Australia, 27; Nationals, 5; Country Liberal Party, 1)
- Australian Labor Party: 25
- Australian Greens: 10
- Australian Motoring Enthusiast Party: 1
- Family First Party: 1
- Liberal Democratic Party: 1
- Palmer United Party: 3
- Independents: 4

C. Role of the Speaker of the House of Representatives

Under section 35 of the Constitution, the House of Representatives must elect a member to be the Speaker of the House. The Speaker is commonly referred to as the "presiding officer" as he or she chairs meetings of the House. The Speaker is also the spokesperson for the House in relation to the other parts of the Parliament, the other branches of government, and outside entities. He or she has ultimate responsibility for the administration of the House, "with a similar role to that of a Minister of State in relation to a government department."[37]

The speakership in Australia is seen as an impartial role. The Parliament website states that "Members are entitled to expect that, even though the Speaker belongs to and is nominated to the position by a political party, his or her functions will be carried out impartially. At the same time, a Speaker is entitled to expect support from all Members regardless of their party."[38]

The Speaker cannot vote on a matter before the House unless the vote is tied, in which case he or she casts a deciding vote.

D. Role of the President of the Senate

The counterpart of the Speaker in the Senate is the President of the Senate. Section 17 of the Constitution requires the Senate to choose a senator to be the President of the Senate. In practice, the President is elected by secret ballot, and the current convention is that presidents are elected from the governing party, even if the government does not have a majority in the Senate. However, the duties of the President, both within and outside the chamber, must be carried out in an impartial manner.[39]

As with the Speaker of the House, the President of the Senate has duties as the presiding officer in meetings of the Senate, as well as having administrative responsibilities in relation to the

---

[37] *House of Representatives Infosheet 3 – The Speaker*, PARLIAMENT OF AUSTRALIA (Aug. 2015), http://www.aph.gov.au/About_Parliament/House_of_Representatives/Powers_practice_and_procedure/00_-_Infosheets/Infosheet_3_-_The_Speaker, *archived at* http://perma.cc/8JPH-L5VV.

[38] *Id.*

[39] ODGERS' AUSTRALIAN SENATE PRACTICE, *supra* note 20, ch. 1 ("The President of the Senate").

Department of the Senate.[40] Section 23 of the Constitution states that "[t]he President shall in all cases be entitled to a vote; and when the votes are equal the question shall pass in the negative." This means that the President's vote carries the same weight as all other senators, thereby maintaining the equal representation of the states in the Senate.

E. Other Parliamentary Officers

In addition to the two presiding officers, there are a range of parliamentary officers in the House and Senate. In the House, this includes the Leader of the House, who is a minister with "overall charge of the arrangement and management of government business in the House."[41] There are also government and opposition whips, who ensure attendance of members and arrange the number and order of their party's speakers in debates.

In terms of nonmembers, key parliamentary officials include the Clerk of the House, "the only non-member to have a speaking role in the proceedings of the House."[42] The Clerk has various procedural functions in the chamber and provides advice to the Speaker and members on "the interpretation of the standing orders, parliamentary practice and precedent, and the requirements of the Constitution and the law affecting the Parliament and the House."[43] Other staff include the Serjeant-at-Arms (who has administrative and security functions), chamber attendants (who distribute bills and other documents to members in the chamber), and Hansard staff (who are responsible for producing a written record of proceedings).[44]

In the Senate, nonmember parliamentary officers include the Clerk of the Senate and the Usher of the Black Rod.[45] This latter position is responsible for various procedural, administrative, and security matters.[46]

---

[40] *Senate Brief No. 6 – The President of the Senate*, PARLIAMENT OF AUSTRALIA (July 2014), http://www.aph.gov.au/About_Parliament/Senate/Powers_practice_n_procedures/Senate_Briefs/Brief06, *archived at* http://perma.cc/SA7P-ZTGJ.

[41] *House of Representatives Infosheet 19 – Government and Opposition*, *supra* note 19.

[42] *House of Representatives Infosheet 21 – The Clerk and Other Officials*, PARLIAMENT OF AUSTRALIA (Feb. 2014), http://www.aph.gov.au/About_Parliament/House_of_Representatives/Powers_practice_and_procedure/00_-_Infosheets/Infosheet_21_-_The_Clerk_and_other_officials, *archived at* http://perma.cc/W4HW-J4AV.

[43] *Id.*

[44] *Id.*

[45] *Senate Brief No. 15 – The Clerk of the Senate and Other Senate Officers*, PARLIAMENT OF AUSTRALIA (July 2014), http://www.aph.gov.au/About_Parliament/Senate/Powers_practice_n_procedures/Senate_Briefs/Brief15, *archived at* http://perma.cc/RH4M-LHPF.

[46] *Senate Brief No. 16 – Usher of the Black Rod*, PARLIAMENT OF AUSTRALIA (July 2014), http://www.aph.gov.au/About_Parliament/Senate/Powers_practice_n_procedures/Senate_Briefs/Brief16, *archived at* http://perma.cc/5B8C-7JK9.

F. Parliamentary Committees

1. Overview

Both government and nongovernment members of the two houses are appointed to various parliamentary committees, which are tasked with investigating "specific matters of policy or government administration or performance."[47]

There are two broad types of committee: select committees, which are created by resolution as required "to inquire into and report on" a specific issue, and standing committees, which are appointed at the beginning of each Parliament.[48] In the House of Representatives, there are several standing "investigative committees," which "carry out inquiries on matters of public policy or government administration."[49] In the Senate, there is a system involving "legislative scrutiny" standing committees and "legislative and general purpose" standing committees. These latter committees are currently structured in pairs—a references committee and a legislation committee—for each subject area.[50] In addition, the standing committees of both houses include domestic or internal committees, which are concerned with the internal operations of the relevant house. Other types of committees are estimates committees and joint committees.

The general committee process involves the development of terms of reference for each committee "inquiry"; these may be referred to the committee by the relevant house, by a minister, by a law, or developed by the committee itself, depending on the type of committee. The terms of reference are then publicized and the committee invites people and organizations to send in "submissions." The committee may invite submitters to attend a public hearing where they will discuss their submissions and answer questions. Public hearings "are often held away from Canberra, in State capitals and regional centres and sometimes by videoconference."[51] After considering the evidence, the committee prepares a report containing conclusions and recommendations, which is presented to the relevant house. Dissenting views of members may be included in a minority or dissenting report attached to the main report.

2. House Committees

Current House committees include standing investigative committees on agriculture and industry; appropriations and administration; communications and the arts; economics; education and employment; the environment; health; indigenous affairs; infrastructure, transport and cities;

---

[47] *House of Representatives Infosheet 4 – Committees*, PARLIAMENT OF AUSTRALIA (Feb. 2014), http://www.aph.gov.au/About_Parliament/House_of_Representatives/Powers_practice_and_procedure/00_-_Infosheets/Infosheet_4_-_Committees, *archived at* http://perma.cc/5PQM-HEW3.

[48] *Senate Brief No. 4 – Committees*, PARLIAMENT OF AUSTRALIA (Sept. 2015), http://www.aph.gov.au/Home/About%20Parliament/Senate/Powers%20practice%20n%20procedures/Senate%20Briefs/Brief04, *archived at* http://perma.cc/9XQY-5WZL.

[49] *About the House of Representatives*, *supra* note 30.

[50] *Senate Brief No. 4 – Committees*, *supra* note 48.

[51] *House of Representatives Infosheet 4 – Committees*, *supra* note 47.

petitions; social policy and legal affairs; and tax and revenue.[52] There are internal standing committees for privileges and members' interests, procedure, publications, and selection (a committee established to "determine the program of business for committee and delegation business and private Members' business for each sitting Monday, to select bills for referral to committees, and set speaking times for second reading debates."[53]).

3. Senate Committees

The two Senate legislative scrutiny committees are the Scrutiny of Bills Committee and the Regulations and Ordinances Committee. All bills and subordinate legislative instruments that come before Parliament are scrutinized by one of these committees "to ensure they conform to certain principles mainly concerned with civil liberties."[54]

The subject areas for the standing legislative and general purpose committees are community affairs; economics; education and employment; environment and communications; finance and public administration; foreign affairs, defense and trade; health; legal and constitutional affairs; and rural and regional affairs and transport.[55] As noted above, for each subject there is a legislation committee and a references committee.

The domestic committees cover privileges; procedure; publications; selection of bills; senators' interests; appropriations and staffing; and library.[56] There are currently three Senate select committees, on the Murray-Darling Basin Plan, the National Broadband Network, and unconventional gas mining.

4. Joint Committees

There are currently nineteen joint committees. Joint standing committees include those covering electoral matters; foreign affairs, defense and trade; migration; the national capital and external territories; the National Disability Insurance Scheme; the parliamentary library; public accounts and audit; public works; and treaties.[57] Under resolutions of the current Parliament, joint select committees have been established on the Australia Fund Establishment, Northern Australia, and trade and investment growth. There are several joint committees that have been established pursuant to specific legislative provisions, including committees on the Australian Commission

---

[52] *House of Representatives Committees: House Committees of the 44th Parliament*, PARLIAMENT OF AUSTRALIA, http://www.aph.gov.au/Parliamentary_Business/Committees/House_of_Representatives_Committees?url=comm_lis t_htm (last visited Nov. 27, 2015), *archived at* http://perma.cc/Z6SA-5BB8.

[53] *Selection Committee*, PARLIAMENT OF AUSTRALIA, http://www.aph.gov.au/Parliamentary_Business/Committees/ House/Selection (last visited Nov. 27, 2015), *archived at* http://perma.cc/2QYZ-MP5C.

[54] *Senate Brief No. 4 – Committees*, *supra* note 48.

[55] *Senate Committees*, PARLIAMENT OF AUSTRALIA, http://www.aph.gov.au/Parliamentary_Business/Committees/ Senate (last visited Nov. 27, 2015), *archived at* http://perma.cc/XL93-9YD3.

[56] ODGERS' AUSTRALIAN SENATE PRACTICE, *supra* note 20, ch. 16 ("Standing Domestic Committees").

[57] *Joint Committees*, PARLIAMENT OF AUSTRALIA, http://www.aph.gov.au/Parliamentary_Business/Committees/Joint (last visited Nov. 27, 2015), *archived at* http://perma.cc/655S-YBVC.

for Law Enforcement Integrity, broadcasting of parliamentary proceedings, corporations and financial services, human rights, intelligence and security, and law enforcement.

5. Estimates Committees

There are eight Senate legislation committees to which the government's estimates of proposed annual expenditure of government departments are referred for examination. This referral occurs twice per year—after the introduction of appropriation bills in the House in May and then later in the year when additional estimates are introduced into Parliament.[58] The committees are established at the beginning of each Parliament and consist of three government members, two opposition members, and a member from the minority parties or independent senators. They hold hearings over several days, during which ministers and officials from the relevant department or agency answer questions from the committee. The committees then present their reports to the Senate.

The House of Representatives does not have equivalent committees to the Senate estimates committees. Instead, it "considers the proposed expenditures in the House itself during the consideration in detail stage and does not question government officials directly."[59]

IV. Elections

A. Overview

Elections for the federal Parliament take place every three years, at which time all of the members of the House are elected, and half of the Senate. While state senators have a fixed term of six years, starting on July 1 and ending on June 30 six years later, each House of Representatives has a maximum term of three years from its first meeting after an election but may be dissolved at any time by the Governor-General, acting on the advice of the Prime Minister.[60] Therefore, an early dissolution of the House can lead to the Senate and House elections being desynchronized. This happened between 1963 and 1974 but has since been avoided.[61] Depending on the timing of the elections, there can be some delay before the new Senate commences on July 1.

The Prime Minister decides the date for a House of Representatives election. Once the term of the House expires or the House is dissolved, the Governor-General issues the "writs" for the

---

[58] *Senate Brief No. 5 – Consideration of Estimates by the Senate's Legislation Committees*, PARLIAMENT OF AUSTRALIA (July 2014), http://www.aph.gov.au/About_Parliament/Senate/Powers_practice_n_procedures/ Senate_Briefs/Brief05, *archived at* http://perma.cc/4SSL-ZA4Q.

[59] *House of Representatives Infosheet 10 – The Budget and Financial Legislation*, PARLIAMENT OF AUSTRALIA (Feb. 2014), http://www.aph.gov.au/About_Parliament/House_of_Representatives/Powers_practice_and_procedure/00_- _Infosheets/Infosheet_10_-_Budget_and_financial_legislation, *archived at* http://perma.cc/E2L8-VLAN.

[60] *Elections*, PARLIAMENT OF AUSTRALIA, http://www.aph.gov.au/About_Parliament/Work_of_the_Parliament/ Elections/Elections (last visited Nov. 27, 2015), *archived at* http://perma.cc/F6EH-6TYB.

[61] *Id.*

election. Electoral writs command "an electoral officer to hold an election and contains dates for the close of rolls, the close of nominations, polling day and the return of the writ."[62]

Federal elections are run by the Australian Electoral Commission. The most recent federal elections for the House and Senate took place on September 7, 2013.[63] The next House of Representatives election must be held before January 14, 2017. The Australian Election Commission further explains that

> [t]he terms of senators elected for six years in 2010 expire on 30 June 2017. The earliest possible date for the next half-Senate election is 6 August 2016 and the latest possible date is 13 May 2017.
>
> The earliest possible date for the next simultaneous House of Representatives and half-Senate election is 6 August 2016 and the latest possible date is 14 January 2017.[64]

There are no limits on the number of times senators and members (including a Prime Minister) may stand for election to the federal Parliament.[65]

All eligible Australian citizens aged eighteen years and over are required to enroll to vote. In addition, voting in federal elections is compulsory for all enrolled voters.[66] As a result, voter turnout is very high. In the 2013 elections, turnout was 93.88% and 93.23% for the Senate and House elections respectively.[67]

B. Elections for the House of Representatives

As noted above, there are 150 electoral divisions in Australia, each of which elects one member of the House of Representatives. Each division has an average population of 150,000 citizens, with an average of 100,000 voters.[68]

---

[62] *Federal Election Timetable*, AUSTRALIAN ELECTORAL COMMISSION, http://www.aec.gov.au/elections/australian_electoral_system/electoral_procedures/Federal_Election_Timetable htm (last updated Mar. 25, 2013), *archived at* http://perma.cc/53JX-XPCH.

[63] *Federal, State and Territory Election Dates from 1946 to Present*, AUSTRALIAN ELECTORAL COMMISSION, http://www.aec.gov.au/Elections/Australian_Electoral_History/Federal_State_and_Territory_elections_dates_1946_Present.htm (last updated May 26, 2015), *archived at* http://perma.cc/5GZH-TNLR.

[64] *Elections – Frequently Asked Questions*, AUSTRALIAN ELECTORAL COMMISSION, http://www.aec.gov.au/faqs/Elections.htm (last updated Aug. 7, 2014), *archived at* http://perma.cc/N9JE-QZW7.

[65] Martin Lumb, *The 43rd Parliament: Traits and Trends*, AUSTRALIAN PARLIAMENTARY LIBRARY (Oct. 2, 2013), http://www.aph.gov.au/About_Parliament/Parliamentary_Departments/Parliamentary_Library/pubs/rp/rp1314/43rdParl, *archived at* http://perma.cc/2Q5G-3S4J.

[66] *Voting*, PARLIAMENT OF AUSTRALIA, http://www.aec.gov.au/Voting/index htm (last updated May 30, 2013), *archived at* http://perma.cc/BGS4-L7PD.

[67] *Who Voted in Previous Referendums and Elections*, AUSTRALIAN ELECTORAL COMMISSION, http://www.aec.gov.au/Elections/Australian_Electoral_History/Voter_Turnout.htm (last updated Sept. 9, 2015), *archived at* http://perma.cc/CWG5-4Q2N.

[68] *Federal Elections*, PARLIAMENTARY EDUCATION OFFICE, http://www.peo.gov.au/learning/fact-sheets/federal-elections.html (last visited Nov. 27, 2015), *archived at* http://perma.cc/6BG7-ZS8P.

Elections for the House of Representatives utilize a full preferential voting system, which involves voters ranking all candidates standing in their electoral division in order of preference. This is done by placing numbers in the boxes opposite the candidates' names, which are listed in random order. To be successful, "a candidate must be supported by a majority (that is, more than half) of voters."[69] The vote counting works as follows:

> First, all of the number '1' votes are counted for each candidate. If a candidate gets more than half the total first preference votes, that candidate will be elected.
>
> If no candidate has more than half of the votes, the candidate with the fewest votes is excluded. This candidate's votes are transferred to the other candidates according to the second preferences of voters on the ballot papers for the excluded candidate. If still no candidate has more than half the votes, the candidate who now has the fewest votes is excluded and the votes are transferred according to the next preference shown. This process continues until one candidate has more than half the total number of formal votes and is elected.[70]

C. Elections for the Senate

Since 1948, senators have also been elected using a preferential or ranked voting system. However, different from those for the House of Representatives, Senate elections utilize a more complicated single transferable vote system to achieve proportional representation. This system "ensures that political parties gain representation in proportion to their share of the vote."[71] The twelve candidates elected from each state are the ones that have "obtained a number of votes equal to or exceeding a required quota (or proportion of votes) necessary for election."[72] The system may be summarized as follows:

> The quota is obtained by dividing the total number of formal votes by one more than the number of candidates to be elected, and adding one to the result. Thus, if the total of formal votes in a state at an election for six senators is 700 000, the quota is 100 001. That is, a candidate will need to win at least 100 001 votes to be elected.
>
> Candidates receiving votes in excess of the quota, which is a proportion rather than a majority of the total vote, have their surplus votes distributed according to their electors' ranking of preferences. If all the positions have not then been filled by candidates obtaining quotas by this means, then the next preferences of the voters for the least

---

[69] *House of Representatives Infosheet 8 – Elections for the House of Representatives*, PARLIAMENT OF AUSTRALIA (Feb. 2014), http://www.aph.gov.au/About_Parliament/House_of_Representatives/Powers_practice_and_procedure/00_-_Infosheets/Infosheet_8_-_Elections_for_the_House_of_Representatives, *archived at* http://perma.cc/BQA8-8MNB.

[70] *Counting the Votes for the House of Representatives*, AUSTRALIAN ELECTORAL COMMISSION, http://www.aec.gov.au/Voting/counting/hor_count.htm (last updated July 17, 2015), *archived at* http://perma.cc/4ZG7-JYJQ.

[71] *Senate Brief No. 1 – Electing Australia's Senators*, PARLIAMENT OF AUSTRALIA (July 2014), http://www.aph.gov.au/About_Parliament/Senate/Powers_practice_n_procedures/Senate_Briefs/Brief01, *archived at* http://perma.cc/ZK45-56RA.

[72] *Id.*

successful candidates are distributed, until all vacancies are filled by candidates obtaining quotas. The end result is a constituency with several candidates elected, each representing a proportion or quota of the total vote.[73]

The counting of first preferences begins on election night; however, "the full count cannot be completed until several weeks after the election."[74]

V. Legislative Process

A. Standard Process

For standard government bills, not related to appropriations or taxation, the policies may originate from different sources. Regardless of the source, legislative proposals are considered by the Cabinet or the Prime Minister. If a proposal is agreed to, the responsible minister directs the relevant government department to arrange preparation of the bill. All government bills are drafted by the Office of Parliamentary Counsel based on detailed instructions developed by a department.[75]

Where a government bill is to be introduced in the House, as in the great majority of cases, the responsible minister gives written notice to the Clerk of the House of his or her intention to introduce the bill. It is then included on the Notice Paper for the next sitting day. The following steps are taken in introducing, debating, and passing a government bill:

- First Reading: After the Clerk announces the item on the Notice Paper and reads the title of the bill, the minister stands and says "I present the . . . Bill" and hands a signed copy of the bill to the Clerk. All government bills are accompanied by an explanatory memorandum, which explains the reasons for the bill and provides an outline of its provisions. The Clerk then stands and reads out the "long title" of the bill, which "sets out in very broad terms the purpose or scope of the bill." This is called the "first reading."[76]

- Second Reading: Usually immediately after the first reading, the minister moves that the bill "now be read a second time." He or she then "makes a speech (second reading speech) explaining the purpose, general principles and effect of the bill." Debate on the bill is then adjourned and "set down as an item of business for a future sitting."[77]

- Second Reading Debate: The second reading debate usually takes place after several sitting days, depending on the government's legislative program and negotiation with the opposition. When the debate resumes, an opposition member outlines the opposition's position on the bill, then government and opposition members speak in turn. The second

---

[73] *Id. See also* ODGERS' AUSTRALIAN SENATE PRACTICE, *supra* note 20, ch. 4.

[74] *Counting the Votes for the Senate*, AUSTRALIAN ELECTORAL COMMISSION, http://www.aec.gov.au/voting/counting/senate_count.htm (last updated July 17, 2015), *archived at* http://perma.cc/82RA-JQTM.

[75] *House of Representatives Infosheet 7 – Making Laws, supra* note 27; HOUSE OF REPRESENTATIVES PRACTICE, *supra* note 8, ch. 10.

[76] *House of Representatives Infosheet 7 – Making Laws, supra* note 27.

[77] *Id.*

reading debate "is normally the most substantial debate that takes place on a bill."[78] At the end of the debate, the minister moves the motion "that this bill be now read a second time." A vote is taken to determine whether the House agrees with the bill in principle, thus completing the second reading.

- Reference to a Committee: A bill may be referred to the relevant House committee for consideration and preparation of an advisory report. The committee can only recommend amendments; it cannot amend the bill itself. If the recommendations are accepted by the government they are incorporated into any government amendments that are moved during the "consideration in detail" stage of the process.

- Consideration in Detail: At this stage, the text of the bill is considered in detail, clause by clause. This involves brief speeches on individual or groups of clauses, and on any amendments moved by members. Votes are taken at various points during the proceedings to indicate whether there is agreement to clauses and amendments.

- Third Reading: In practice, following the consideration-in-detail stage, the minister is able to move the motion "that this bill be read a third time." There is rarely debate at this stage. When the motion is agreed to, the Clerk reads out the long title of the bill, signifying that the bill has passed the House.

- Transmission to the Senate: After the bill has passed the House, the bill is transmitted to the Senate, with appropriate messages by the Clerk or the Speaker attached.

- Senate Proceedings: The bill also goes through three readings in the Senate. The process involves the first reading; second reading policy debate; reference to a legislation committee (at any point), which reports recommendations back to the Senate; detailed consideration of the bill (this stage is referred to as the Committee of the Whole Senate, or just "committee of the whole"); and third reading (signifying final agreement).[79]

- Royal Assent: After a bill has been passed by the House and Senate in identical form it is presented to the Governor-General for assent. The Constitution does allow the Governor-General to withhold assent, "but in practice a bill passed by both houses is always assented to."[80]

Where there is disagreement between the two houses regarding a bill, "messages may pass between the two Houses to reach agreement as to the bill's final form."[81] Where the negotiations on amendments resolve the disagreement, the bill is voted on in both houses. If there is no agreement, the bill may be laid aside and not proceeded with. It is possible, though very rare, for

---

[78] *Id.*

[79] *Senate Brief No. 8 – The Senate and Legislation*, PARLIAMENT OF AUSTRALIA (Aug. 2015), http://www.aph.gov.au/About_Parliament/Senate/Powers_practice_n_procedures/Senate_Briefs/Brief08, *archived at* http://perma.cc/2656-H2UN; ODGERS' AUSTRALIAN SENATE PRACTICE, *supra* note 20, ch. 12; *Brief Guides to Senate Procedure No. 16 – Consideration of Legislation*, PARLIAMENT OF AUSTRALIA, http://www.aph.gov.au/About_Parliament/Senate/Powers_practice_n_procedures/Brief_Guides_to_Senate_Procedure/No_16 (last reviewed July 2015), *archived at* http://perma.cc/95X9-9LCJ.

[80] *House of Representatives Infosheet 7 – Making Laws*, *supra* note 27.

[81] *Id.*

a disagreement to trigger a "double dissolution," whereby both houses are dissolved and general elections held.[82] The conditions that must be satisfied for this to occur are set out in section 57 of the Constitution. After the election, if the same bill is introduced again and fails to pass the Senate, a joint sitting of both houses, where they vote as one house, may be held.[83]

Note that in the Australian party system, in accordance with the Westminster tradition, members of Parliament "nearly always vote along party lines."[84] The main exception is where the major parties decide to allow members a "conscience vote," where individual members can vote freely according to their own judgment or belief (also called a "free vote").[85] This is used for bills on a small number of moral or social issues, such as abortion and euthanasia. It is also possible for members to "cross the floor" to vote with the opposing parties, or to abstain from voting. Such actions are very rare.

B. Private Members' and Senators' Bills

Time is allocated in the House and Senate for various nongovernment business. This includes the introduction and debate of private members' or senators' bills, which are prepared by opposition or nonaligned members and by government members outside the party's formal approval mechanisms. They must go through the same legislative stages as government bills. Private members' bills are "a small proportion of legislation dealt with by the House" and rarely pass;[86] this is similar in the Senate. They are used by members to signify that they consider debate and legislative action is necessary on an issue. Some may lead to matters being addressed in government bills.

---

[82] *Senate Brief No. 8 – The Senate and Legislation, supra* note 79.

[83] *Senate Brief No. 7 – Disagreement Between the Houses*, PARLIAMENT OF AUSTRALIA (Feb. 2013), http://www.aph.gov.au/About_Parliament/Senate/Powers_practice_n_procedures/Senate_Briefs/Brief07, *archived at* http://perma.cc/VGY8-PRUD.

[84] Deidre McKeown & Rob Lundie, *Free Votes in Australian and Some Overseas Parliaments* (Australian Parliamentary Library, Current Issues Brief No. 1, Aug. 27, 2002), PARLIAMENT OF AUSTRALIA, http://www.aph.gov.au/About_Parliament/Parliamentary_Departments/Parliamentary_Library/Publications_Archive/CIB/cib0203/03CIB01, *archived at* http://perma.cc/7LC8-RCHV.

[85] *See* definition of "Free vote," *Glossary*, PARLIAMENT OF AUSTRALIA, http://www.aph.gov.au/help/glossary#F (last visited Nov. 27, 2015), *archived at* http://perma.cc/9V3C-5NLR.

[86] *House of Representatives Infosheet 6 – Opportunities for Private Members*, PARLIAMENT OF AUSTRALIA (May 2014), http://www.aph.gov.au/About_Parliament/House_of_Representatives/Powers_practice_and_procedure/00_-_Infosheets/Infosheet_6_-_Opportunities_for_private_Members, *archived at* http://perma.cc/9R2M-Z7NE.

Canada

Tariq Ahmad
Foreign law Specialist

SUMMARY   The Canadian Parliament was established in 1867 following the passage, by the British Parliament, of the British North America Act, also referred to in Canada as the Constitution Act, 1867. Canada's Parliament buildings were built between 1859 and 1866 and are located in the seat of the federal government, the City of Ottawa.

Canada is a constitutional monarchy with a parliamentary system of government. The Parliament, which is the federal legislature, is made up of three constitutive parts: the Crown, the Senate, and the House of Commons. Members of the **338-seat** House of Commons are elected through a first-past-the-post electoral system. Some of the important leadership roles in both houses of Parliament are the speakers, house leaders, and whips.

In order for a bill to become law, a multistage process occurs in each house of Parliament, which includes three readings of a bill, followed by Royal Assent.

I. Background

The Canadian Parliament was established pursuant to the British North America Act,[1] also called the Constitution Act, 1867, an Act of the British Parliament that created the Dominion of Canada by joining three British colonies in North America—Nova Scotia, New Brunswick, and Canada—into a Confederation.[2] On December 11, 1931, the Statute of Westminster,[3] also an Act of the British Parliament, allowed complete legislative self-rule (excluding those subject areas that they elected to have remain subordinate to Britain[4]) for what were then the dominions of Canada, Australia, New Zealand, South Africa, Ireland, and Newfoundland. According to Historica Canada, "[a]fter consultation between Canada's federal and provincial governments, the repeal, amendment or alteration of the British North America Acts, 1867–1930—Canada's Constitution—was specifically excepted from the terms of the statute."[5] It was not until March 25, 1982, with the British Parliament's passage of the Canada Act,[6] also called the Constitution

---

[1] British North America Act 1867, c. 3, § 2, http://www.legislation.gov.uk/ukpga/Vict/30-31/3/crossheading/iiunion-declaration-of-union/enacted, *archived at* https://perma.cc/V2XC-XGK7.

[2] *Id.*

[3] Statute of Westminster, 1931, c. 4, http://www.legislation.gov.uk/ukpga/Geo5/22-23/4/section/7/enactedm, *archived at* https://perma.cc/H2ET-M7B9.

[4] *Id.* § 7.

[5] *Statute of Westminster*, HISTORICA CANADA: CANADIAN ENCYCLOPEDIA, http://www.thecanadianencyclopedia.ca/en/article/statute-of-westminster/, *archived at* https://perma.cc/24Q5-EMUS.

[6] Canada Act 1982 (UK), 1982, c. 11, http://www.legislation.gov.uk/ukpga/1982/11/pdfs/ukpga_19820011_en.pdf, *archived at* https://perma.cc/J4QB-MEPA.

Act of 1982, that the power of the UK Parliament to legislate for Canada was officially terminated.[7]

The present-day seat of the federal government, the City of Ottawa, used to be the seat of government of the Province of Canada,[8] and then the Dominion of Canada in 1867.

The seat of government of the Province of Canada alternated for many years.[9] In 1857, Queen Victoria "was asked to select a permanent capital"[10] and she chose the town of Ottawa. According to the Parliament of Canada website, "[t]he Centre, East and West blocks of the Parliament Buildings were built between 1859 and 1866 (excluding the Tower and Library)."[11]

On the night of February 3, 1916, a fire broke out in the Centre block's House of Commons reading room. According to Historica Canada, "[a]ll that remained the following morning were the building's exterior walls and the Parliamentary Library. Rumored to be an act of sabotage, as Canada's energies were focused on war in Europe, the fire was simply an unfortunate accident and caused great alarm within the federal government."[12]

II. Constitutional Status and Role

Canada is a constitutional monarchy with a parliamentary system of government.[13] Canada's Parliament is a federal legislature "composed of individuals selected to represent the Canadian people."[14] It forms the legislative branch of government. The Prime Minister, as head of government, and the Cabinet[15] comprise the executive branch, and Canada's courts at both the federal and provincial levels[16] make up the judicial branch of government. The British monarch

---

[7] *Id.* § 2.

[8] In 1841, Lower Canada, now known as Quebec, and Upper Canada, now known as Ontario, joined to form the Province of Canada.

[9] *The Parliament Buildings*, PARLIAMENT OF CANADA, http://www.parl.gc.ca/about/parliament/publications/parliamentbuildings/parlblgs-e.asp (last updated Dec. 2006), *archived at* https://perma.cc/Q27S-JLQY.

[10] *Id.*

[11] *Id.*

[12] *Parliament Buildings*, HISTORICA CANADA: CANADIAN ENCYCLOPEDIA, http://www.thecanadianencyclopedia.ca/en/article/parliament-buildings/, *archived at* https://perma.cc/C8UN-PM2C.

[13] *Parliamentary Institutions, in* HOUSE OF COMMONS PROCEDURE AND PRACTICE (Robert Marleau & Camille Montpetit eds., 2000), http://www.parl.gc.ca/marleaumontpetit/DocumentViewer.aspx?Sec=Ch01&Seq=2&Language=E, *archived at* https://perma.cc/P8S5-URLE.

[14] *Id.*

[15] Lorraine Snyder & Dustin Martin, *The Constitution and Canada's Branches of Government*, CENTRE FOR CONSTITUTIONAL STUDIES (Apr. 2, 2015), http://ualawccsprod.srv.ualberta.ca/ccs/index.php/constitutional-issues/democratic-governance/818-the-constitution-and-canada-s-branches-of-government, *archived at* https://perma.cc/K8UY-DBMX.

[16] *Id.*

is the head of state and is represented at the federal level in Canada by the Governor General and at the provincial level by lieutenant governors.[17]

The Parliament of Canada shares its law-making function with ten provincial and three territorial governments.[18] The legislative powers of the federal Parliament are stipulated by section 91 of the Constitution Act, 1867.[19] Generally, it has jurisdiction to make laws "for the Peace, Order, and good Government of Canada,"[20] which do not fall within the exclusive legislative authority of the provinces. More specifically, section 91 enumerates classes of subjects on which the federal Parliament has exclusive authority to legislate, including but not limited to the regulation of trade and commerce, military and defense, marriage and divorce, and criminal law.[21]

III. Structure and Composition

A. Senators and Members

Canada's federal legislative branch consists of the monarch, the House of Commons, and the Senate.[22] The Senate and House of Commons constitute Canada's bicameral Parliament.[23] The Senate has 105 members[24] who are appointed by the Governor General on the recommendation of the Prime Minister,[25] while the House of Commons has 338 elected members.[26] Senators are appointed according to four geographical divisions set out in the Constitution Act, 1867.[27] They must own property and live in the relevant division.[28] While they were previously appointed for life, senators now serve until the age of 75.[29]

---

[17] *Id.*

[18] *Parliamentary Institutions, supra note 13.*

[19] Constitution Act, 1867, 30 & 31 Victoria, c. 3 (U.K.), § 91, http://laws-lois.justice.gc.ca/eng/Const//page-4.html#docCont, *archived at* https://perma.cc/K6NM-UYE2.

[20] *Id.*

[21] *Id.*

[22] Snyder & Martin, *supra note 15.*

[23] *Id.*

[24] Constitution Act, 1867, § 21.

[25] *Guide to the Canadian House of Commons: The Canadian Parliament*, PARLIAMENT OF CANADA, http://www.parl.gc.ca/about/parliament/guidetohoc/index-e.htm (last updated Dec. 2011), *archived at* https://perma.cc/LJU9-ZZXZ.

[26] *Id.* Section 37 of the Constitution Act, 1867 stipulates that the House of Commons has 308 members, which was expanded to 338 on December 16, 2011, pursuant to the Fair Representation Act, S.C. 2011, c. 26, http://laws-lois.justice.gc.ca/eng/annualstatutes/2011_26/FullText.html, *archived at* https://perma.cc/N2PM-BNW9.

[27] Constitution Act, 1867, § 22.

[28] *Id.* § 23.

[29] *Id.* § 29(2).

If a political party is able to receive more than half of the total number of seats in the House of Commons it will have a majority government.[30] If a party "wins half or less than half of the seats in the House of Commons but has a plurality (the most seats)" then a minority government is possible if it is able to command the confidence of the House of Commons.[31] The governing party must therefore receive the approval from members of other parties or independents in order to govern.[32] Minority governments are relatively uncommon in Canada due to the adoption of a plurality voting system instead a proportional representation system.

There are currently three recognized political parties[33] in the House of Commons: the New Democratic Party (NDP) (44 members), the Conservative Party (99 members), and the Liberal Party (184 members).[34] Two other parties are represented, but do not have the 12 members needed to be a recognized party for the purposes of parliamentary proceedings: BLOC Québécois (10 members) and the Green Party (one member).[35]

Senators are also usually affiliated with a political party. There are currently two parties represented in the Senate: the Conservative Party (45 senators) and the Liberal Party (28 senators). There are also ten independent senators.[36] Twenty-two seats are currently vacant. The new Liberal government, elected in October 2015, is establishing a board to recommend candidates to fill the vacancies.[37]

B. Leadership Roles

Some of the important leadership roles in both houses of Parliament are the speakers, house leaders, and whips. The Speaker of the House of Commons "presides over the House of Commons and ensures that everyone respects its rules and traditions."[38] The Speaker is voted on

---

[30] *Glossary of Parliamentary Terms for Younger Students*, PARLIAMENT OF CANADA, http://www.parl.gc.ca/About/Parliament/Education/GlossaryElementary/index.asp?Language=E (last updated Feb. 2005), *archived at* https://perma.cc/E9XG-QB8J.

[31] *Minority Government*, THE CANADIAN ENCYCLOPEDIA, http://www.thecanadianencyclopedia.ca/en/article/minority-government/ (last visited Dec. 8, 2015), *archived at* https://perma.cc/Q4A9-S5NM.

[32] *Id.*

[33] "A political party must have at least 12 Members in the House of Commons to be a 'recognized party' for the purposes of parliamentary proceedings." *Party Standings in the House of Commons*, PARLIAMENT OF CANADA, http://www.parl.gc.ca/parliamentarians/en/partystandings (last updated Dec. 2011), *archived at* https://perma.cc/9525-BHND.

[34] *Id.*

[35] *Id.*

[36] *Canada's Senators*, PARLIAMENT OF CANADA, http://sen.parl.gc.ca/portal/canada-senators-e htm (last visited Jan. 4, 2016), *archived at* https://perma.cc/8J9C-Q8SR.

[37] Gloria Galloway, *Liberals to Set Up Advisory Board for Senate Nominees, but B.C. Won't Take Part*, THE GLOBE AND MAIL (Dec. 3, 2015), http://www.theglobeandmail.com/news/politics/liberals-setting-up-advisory-board-to-fill-empty-senate-seats/article27577333/, *archived at* https://perma.cc/7UU5-C43M.

[38] *Guide to the Canadian House of Commons: Who's Who in the House*, PARLIAMENT OF CANADA, http://www.parl.gc.ca/about/parliament/guidetohoc/who-e.htm (last updated Dec. 2011), *archived at* https://perma.cc/5Y7V-HKJS.

by a secret ballot by members of the House of Commons after each general election.[39] According to the *Guide to the Canadian House of Commons*, "[t]he Speaker represents the Commons in dealings with the Senate and the Crown. The Speaker is also responsible for the administration of the House and its staff, and has many diplomatic and social duties."[40] In the Senate, the Speaker is appointed by the Governor General on the recommendation of the Prime Minister.[41] According to the Parliament of Canada website, "[t]he Speaker's principal duty is to preside over the Senate's proceedings, ensure the orderly flow of debate, and interpret parliamentary rules, helping the Senate move through its daily business."[42]

Every officially recognized party appoints one member to be its house leader.[43] The house leaders of "all the parties meet regularly to discuss upcoming business in the Commons, how long bills will be debated and when special issues will be discussed."[44] The leader of the governing party in the Senate is appointed by the Prime Minister.[45]

Every officially recognized party also has a whip to "ensure that enough party members are in the Chamber for debates and votes."[46] The whips also "determine which committees a party member will sit on, assign offices and seats in the House, and discipline members who break party ranks."[47] The Senate similarly has party whips "to keep its members up to date on the business and schedule of the Senate and its committees, as well as to ensure the attendance and voting of its members," and to "work to maximize participation when a vote is called in the Senate Chamber, and ensure full participation in committee meetings."[48]

C. Committees

There are several different types of committees that operate in the House of Commons and the Senate,[49] falling into four main categories: standing, special, joint, and committees of the whole.

---

[39] *Id.*

[40] *Id.*

[41] *Senate of Canada Fact Sheet: Key Roles in the Senate*, PARLIAMENT OF CANADA, http://sen.parl.gc.ca/portal/publications/factsheets/fs-keyroles-e htm, *archived at* https://perma.cc/9PNP-ZUMX.

[42] *Id.*

[43] *Guide to the Canadian House of Commons: Who's Who in the House, supra* note 38.

[44] *Id.*

[45] *Senate of Canada Fact Sheet: Key Roles in the Senate, supra* note 41.

[46] *Guide to the Canadian House of Commons: Who's Who in the House, supra* note 38.

[47] *Id.*

[48] *Senate of Canada Fact Sheet: Key Roles in the Senate, supra* note 41.

[49] For a list of Committees in the House of Commons, see *Committees: House of Commons*, PARLIAMENT OF CANADA, http://www.parl.gc.ca/Committees/en/Home, *archived at* https://perma.cc/Z5R5-38G5. For the Senate see *Senate Committees*, PARLIAMENT OF CANADA, http://www.parl.gc.ca/sencommitteebusiness/?Language=E, *archived at* https://perma.cc/QEK7-U9VQ.

Standing committees are permanent committees that are established through standing orders.[50] They typically "correspond broadly to fields of public policy, such as agriculture, banking, fisheries, foreign affairs, energy, Aboriginal affairs, and technology."[51] Special committees are created on an ad hoc basis. They are appointed by an order in council and are authorized to conduct studies on a specific and narrow subject area of interest. When the study is concluded and a final report is submitted to a House of Parliament, the special committee is dissolved.[52] Joint committees, which can be special or standing, "include both senators and members of the House of Commons. These committees are established to examine issues of mutual interest to both Houses of Parliament."[53] Committees of the whole are composed of the entire membership of the Senate or House Chamber.

Subcommittees are also established by standing committees for multiple reasons, and "may exist for the duration of a Parliament or may cease to exist when their specific purpose has been accomplished."[54]

IV. Elections

In order to become a Member of Parliament, namely the House of Commons, a person must run for a seat in the federal elections, which are held on the third Monday in October every four years.[55]

Section 50 of the Constitution Act, 1867 stipulates that general elections of the House of Commons must be held at least once every five years but does not specify any fixed dates.[56] According to the Parliament of Canada website, "[t]raditionally, under a parliamentary system of government, general elections are called at the discretion of the prime minister, although they may be held at any time if the government loses the confidence of the legislature."[57] It was only in 2007 that the Parliament of Canada amended the Canada Elections Act[58] to introduce fixed

---

[50] *Committees*, COMPENDIUM: HOUSE OF COMMONS PROCEDURE ONLINE, PARLIAMENT OF CANADA, http://www. parl.gc.ca/About/House/Compendium/web-content/c_g_committees-e.htm (last updated Feb. 2010), *archived at* https://perma.cc/86UY-DKL9.

[51] *Senate of Canada Fact Sheet: Senate Committees*, PARLIAMENT OF CANADA (2012), http://sen.parl.gc.ca/portal/ publications/factsheets/fs-committees-e.htm, *archived at* https://perma.cc/3RYJ-7Z4D.

[52] *Guide to Government Publications Canada – Committees and Commissions*, MCMASTER UNIVERSITY LIBRARIES, https://library.mcmaster.ca/govpubs/guides/committees_commissions htm, *archived at* https://perma.cc/3RZV-3FXD.

[53] *Senate of Canada Fact Sheet: Senate Committees, supra* note 41.

[54] *Committees, supra* note 50.

[55] Guide to the Canadian House of Commons: The Canadian Parliament, *supra* note 25.

[56] Constitution Act, 1867, § 50.

[57] *Fixed-Date Elections in Canada*, PARLINFO, Parliament of Canada, http://www.parl.gc.ca/parlinfo/compilations/ provinceterritory/ProvincialFixedElections.aspx (last updated Jan. 12, 2015), *archived at* https://perma.cc/4ZZT-ML3Q.

[58] Canada Elections Act, S.C. 2000, c. 9, http://laws-lois.justice.gc.ca/PDF/E-2.01.pdf, *archived at* https://perma.cc/ 3424-F694.

dates for general elections. The 2007 amendment stipulates that each general election must be held on the third Monday of October every four years.[59] According to Eugene Forsey's *How Canadians Govern Themselves*, "[i]n practice this means that the expected term of office for a member of Parliament (or of a legislature with a fixed-date law) would normally be four years. However, the Governor General's power to dissolve Parliament is not affected by the fixed date legislation."[60]

The first fixed-date election was held on October 19, 2015.[61] The previous general election was held on May 2, 2011,[62] after the Prime Minister advised the Governor General to dissolve the Parliament following the passage of a motion of no-confidence in the government. The 2011 election was the fourth federal election in seven years.[63]

Each seat in the House of Commons represents one of the country's 338 constituencies. A candidate need not receive more than half the votes, just a plurality or the most votes to get elected as a member of Parliament.[64] According to the Parliament of Canada website,

> [s]eats in the House of Commons are distributed roughly in proportion to the population of each province and territory. In general, the more people in a province or territory, the more Members it has in the House of Commons. Every province or territory must have at least as many Members in the Commons as it has in the Senate.[65]

By-elections to fill empty seats "are not affected by the introduction of fixed-date elections, and continue to be held between the dates of general elections as required."[66]

Canada's general elections are run based on the "single-member plurality" system (also known as the "first-past-the-post" system).[67] According to Elections Canada,

---

[59] An Act to Amend the Canada Elections Act S.C. 2007, c. 10, § 56.1(2), http://laws-lois.justice.gc.ca/eng/annualstatutes/2007_10/page-1.html, *archived at* https://perma.cc/4N74-SRHN.

[60] EUGENE FORSEY, HOW CANADIANS GOVERN THEMSELVES (8th ed. 2008), http://www.parl.gc.ca/about/parliament/senatoreugeneforsey/book/assets/pdf/How_Canadians_Govern_Themselves8.pdf, *archived at* https://perma.cc/6Y9M-AB9S.

[61] *October 19, 2015, Election Results*, ELECTIONS CANADA, http://enr.elections.ca/National.aspx?lang=e, *archived at* https://perma.cc/26BL-RL7T.

[62] *Past Elections*, ELECTIONS CANADA, http://www.elections.ca/content.aspx?section=ele&dir=pas&document=index&lang=e (last visited Dec. 8, 2015), *archived at* https://perma.cc/VZD8-XWG8.

[63] *Canadian Government Collapses in No-Confidence Vote*, THE GUARDIAN (Mar. 25, 2011), http://www.theguardian.com/world/2011/mar/26/canadian-government-no-confidence-vote, *archived at* https://perma.cc/XN6J-9CZ6.

[64] *Guide to the Canadian House of Commons: The Canadian Parliament*, *supra* note 25.

[65] *Id.*

[66] *Fixed-Date Elections in Canada*, *supra* note 57.

[67] *The Electoral System of Canada*, ELECTIONS CANADA, http://www.elections.ca/content.aspx?dir=ces&document=part1&lang=e&section=res (last visited Dec. 8, 2015), *archived at* https://perma.cc/4WQ3-LP5S.

[i]n every electoral district, the candidate with the highest number of votes wins a seat in the House of Commons and represents that electoral district as its member of Parliament. An absolute majority (more than 50 percent of the votes in the electoral district) is not required for a candidate to be elected.[68]

According to preliminary results from the 2015 general elections, there was a high turnout of 68.49% of registered voters.[69] The previous 2011 election had a voter turnout of 61.1%.[70]

V. Legislative Process

In order for bills to become law in Canada, a long and multistage process occurs in each House of Parliament[71], which includes introduction of a bill, first reading, second reading, committee stage, reporting stage, third reading, and finally Royal Assent.[72] According to the *Compendium*, an online guide to House of Commons procedure, "[a]ll bills must go through the same stages of the legislative process, but they do not necessarily follow the same route."[73] Three possible paths exist for the approval of legislation:

- After appropriate notice, a minister or a member may introduce a bill, which will be given a first reading immediately. The bill is then debated generally at the second reading stage and sent to a committee for clause-by-clause study.

- A minister may move that a bill be referred to a committee for study before a second reading.

- A minister or member may propose a motion that a committee be instructed to prepare a bill. A bill will be presented by the committee and carried through the second reading stage without debate or amendment.[74]

---

[68] *Id.*

[69] *October 19, 2015 Election Results*, ELECTIONS CANADA, http://enr.elections.ca/National.aspx, *archived at* https://perma.cc/86W7-8R96.

[70] *Voter Turnout at Federal Elections and Referendums*, ELECTIONS CANADA, http://www.elections.ca/content. aspx?dir=turn&document=index&lang=e&section=ele, *archived at* https://perma.cc/2TYU-6D2W.

[71] The written rules that regulate the proceedings of the House of Commons are known as Standing Orders of the House of Commons (Oct. 2015), http://www.parl.gc.ca/about/house/standingorders/toc-e.htm, *archived at* https://perma.cc/4UN3-W3H7. Senate proceedings are governed by the Rules of the Senate, http://www.parl.gc.ca/About/Senate/Rules/senrules_00-e.htm, *archived at* https://perma.cc/KW9U-WVXR.

[72] *How a Government Bill Becomes Law – Canada*, QUEEN'S UNIVERSITY LIBRARY, http://library.queensu. ca/gov/bills_federal (last updated Aug. 27, 2014), *archived at* https://perma.cc/25KM-6BWD.

[73] *Legislative Process*, COMPENDIUM: HOUSE OF COMMONS PROCEDURE ONLINE, PARLIAMENT OF CANADA, http://www.parl.gc.ca/About/House/Compendium/web-content/c_g_legislativeprocess-e.htm (last updated Feb. 2010), *archived at* https://perma.cc/VU5D-3DJZ.

[74] *Id.*

A. Types and Forms of Bills

Generally there are three types of bills: new legislation sponsored by government Cabinet ministers and bills that originate from a member of Parliament, which together are considered "public bills"; and bills that originate on the initiative of private parties, or "private bills."[75]

1. Public Bills

a. Government Bills

According to the *Compendium*, "[a] government bill is the text of a legislative initiative that a Minister of the Crown submits to Parliament to be approved, and possibly amended, before becoming law."[76] Bills for appropriations, including the raising of public revenue and taxation, must be introduced by the government in the House of Commons.[77]

Important types of financial bills typically introduced by the government include the following:

- Ways and means bills—which increase or extend the scope of a tax;

- Appropriation bills—which are introduced in the House following the adoption of Main [planned budgets or appropriations] or Supplementary Estimates [adjusted departmental budgets] or Interim Supply [funds required by the Government to conduct its activities from the beginning of the fiscal year to the final supply day] and authorize the withdrawal of funds from the Consolidated Revenue Fund; and

- Borrowing authority bills—which seek authority to borrow money when public revenues are not adequate to cover government expenditures.[78]

Government bills may also address "matters of public interest," and in such cases are permitted to include financial provisions.[79]

b. Private Members' Bills

Private members' bills are introduced by members of Parliament who are not Cabinet ministers.[80] These bills cannot include "financial provisions" or authorization for the expenditure of public funds unless the "Member has sought and been granted a Royal

---

[75] *Bills: The Origin of New Legislation*, BEST GUIDE TO CANADIAN LEGAL RESEARCH, http://legalresearch.org/statutory/federal-statutes/bills, *archived at* https://perma.cc/LCA7-4HJU.

[76] *Types of Bills*, COMPENDIUM: HOUSE OF COMMONS PROCEDURE ONLINE, PARLIAMENT OF CANADA, http://www.parl.gc.ca/About/House/Compendium/web-content/c_d_typesbills-e htm (last updated Feb. 2010), *archived at* https://perma.cc/P5LP-DTDC.

[77] *Id.*

[78] *Id.*

[79] *Id.*

[80] *Id.*

Recommendation." [81]   According to the *Compendium*, "[m]ost private Members' bills are initiated in the House of Commons, but some originate in the Senate.   Debate on private Member's bills takes place during the daily hour set aside for 'Private Members' Business'." [82]

2. Private Bills

Private bills are used to "exempt a person or group of persons, including a corporation from the application of a statute." [83]   Private bills cannot be introduced by a minister, "and must be based on a petition signed by those interested in promoting it." [84]

According to the *Compendium*, "[m]ost private bills are introduced in the Senate, but occasionally, they are introduced in the House of Commons.   Private bills before the House are dealt with as Private Members' Business." [85]   This is because they can only be moved by members who are not part of the ministerial cabinet. [86]

3. Characteristic of Bills According to Purpose

House of Commons Procedure and Practice lists "other drafting characteristics" of bills, which depend on the purpose of the legislation:

- New legislation: Bills resulting from policy decisions or, in some cases, to implement treaties, conventions or agreements, to accept recommendations arising out of a report of a Task Force or Royal Commission of Inquiry, to carry out administrative measures, or to deal with emergencies.

- Major revisions of existing Acts: Bills to revise an Act because it contains a sunset clause (providing that it must be revised after a certain period of time) or because of changing economic or social standards or circumstances.

- Amendments to existing Acts: Bills to amend existing Acts.   The amendments may be either of a substantive or of a housekeeping nature.

- Statute law amendment bills: Initiatives to eliminate anomalies, inconsistencies, archaisms or errors in existing legislation and to deal with other matters of a non-controversial and uncomplicated nature.

- Ways and means bills: Initiatives based on ways and means motions, the purpose of which is to create a new income tax or other taxes, to continue a tax which is expiring, to increase a tax or to extend the scope of a tax.   These bills are governed

---

[81] *Id.*

[82] *Id.*

[83] *Types of Bills, supra* note 76.

[84] *Id.*

[85] *Id.*

[86] *Types of Bills,* HOUSE OF COMMONS PROCEDURE AND PRACTICE (2d ed. 2009), http://www.parl.gc.ca/procedure-book-livre/Document.aspx?sbdid=DA2AC62F-BB39-4E5F-9F7D-90BA3496D0A6&sbpid=51EDABFE-64DD-4BDF-A366-03B3DD6C8375&Language=E&Mode=1, *archived at* https://perma.cc/96D9-GE6C.

by specific provisions of the Standing Orders. Only a Minister may introduce a ways and means bill.

- Appropriation bills: Initiatives introduced in the House in response to the adoption of main or supplementary estimates or interim supply. These bills are also governed by specific provisions of the Standing Orders. Only a Minister may introduce an appropriation bill.

- Borrowing authority bills: Initiatives to seek authority to raise money when public revenues are not adequate to cover government expenditures.

- *Pro forma* bills: A *pro forma* bill is introduced by the Prime Minister at the beginning of each session. It affirms the right of the House to conduct its proceedings and to legislate, regardless of the reasons stated in the Speech from the Throne for convening the House. The bill is entitled *An Act Respecting the Administration of Oaths of Office*; it is numbered C–1 but is not usually printed. It is given first reading, but not second reading.

- Draft bills: This expression is used to refer to the draft form of bills that have not yet been introduced in either House. Occasionally, the House may have the draft of a government bill sent to a committee for examination. As the bill has not yet been given first reading, the committee may examine the proposed legislation without being constrained by the rules of the legislative process, and may recommend changes. The government can then take the committee's report into consideration when finalizing the draft of the bill.

- Omnibus bills: Although this expression is commonly used, there is no precise definition of an omnibus bill. In general, an omnibus bill seeks to amend, repeal or enact several Acts, and is characterized by the fact that it is made up of a number of related but separate initiatives. An omnibus bill has "one basic principle or purpose which ties together all the proposed enactments and thereby renders the Bill intelligible for parliamentary purposes". One of the reasons cited for introducing an omnibus bill is to bring together in a single bill all the legislative amendments arising from a single policy decision in order to facilitate parliamentary debate.[87]

B. Overview of the Process

A federal bill must pass three readings in both the House of Commons and the Senate before it is passed into law.[88] Legislation is typically initiated in the House of Commons, but it can originate in the Senate as well.[89]

---

[87] *Id.*

[88] *See* Chapter IX of *Standing Orders of the House of Commons* for rules on the legislative process by which Public bills are passed in the House of Commons. Standing Order 71 stipulates that "[e]very bill shall receive three several readings, on different days, previously to being passed. On urgent or extraordinary occasions, a bill may be read twice or thrice, or advanced two or more stages in one day." Rules on the legislative process of passing Public Bills in the Senate are provisioned under Chapter 10 of the *Rules of the Senate*.

[89] *Bills: The Origin of New Legislation, supra* note 75.

1. Introduction and First Reading

The first reading is perceived largely as a formality. A written notice of forty-eight hours is required before a public bill can be introduced in the House.[90] According to *House of Commons Procedure and Practice*, once the notice period has elapsed, the bill sponsor, whether a member or minister, takes the following steps:

> [He or She] notifies the Chair of his or her intention to proceed during Routine Proceedings when the rubric "Introduction of Government Bills" (if the sponsor is a Minister) or "Introduction of Private Members' Bills" is called. Leave to introduce a bill is granted automatically, and the motion is deemed carried, without debate, amendment or question put. A Minister seldom provides any explanation when requesting leave to introduce a bill, but may do so. On the other hand, a private Member normally provides a brief explanation of the bill he or she is introducing in the House.[91]

2. Second Reading

The second reading stage "gives Members an opportunity to debate the general scope of the bill."[92] According to the *Compendium*, "[u]nless a bill has been referred to committee prior to second reading, debate at this stage must focus on the principle of the bill and, accordingly, the text of the bill may not be amended before being read a second time and referred to committee."[93] Though traditionally seen as the most important stage, more recently it is seen as less significant. A passage of a motion for second reading of a Bill implies that the "House had given preliminary consideration to the bill, without any commitment to its final passage, and had authorized its reference to a committee for detailed scrutiny and possible amendment."[94] The motion for second reading can be amended. Three types of amendments are allowed:

- a three months' or six months' hoist, which seeks to postpone consideration of the bill for three or six months;

- a reasoned amendment, which requests that the House not give second reading to a bill for a specific reason; or

- a motion to refer the subject matter of the bill to a committee.[95]

---

[90] Standing Orders of the House of Commons (Oct. 2015), Standing Order 54(1).

[91] *Stages in the Legislative Process*, HOUSE OF COMMONS PROCEDURE AND PRACTICE (2d ed. 2009), http://www.parl.gc.ca/procedure-book-livre/document.aspx?sbdid=da2ac62f-bb39-4e5f-9f7d-90ba3496d0a6&sbpidx=6, *archived at* https://perma.cc/PP7C-ZXSW.

[92] *Legislative Process, supra* note 73.

[93] *Id.*

[94] *Stages in the Legislative Process, supra* note 91.

[95] *Legislative Process, supra* note 73.

3. Committee

During the committee stage[96], members have the opportunity to examine and review the clauses of a bill in detail[97] and to approve or modify it.[98] According to *House of Commons Procedure and Practice*,

> [i]t is at this stage that they have their first opportunity to propose amendments to its text. It is also at this stage that witnesses may be invited to present their views and to answer Members' questions. A bill is referred to a standing, special or legislative committee for consideration, normally after second reading in the House, but sometimes before second reading. While any bill based on a supply motion must be referred to a Committee of the Whole, any bill may be referred to a Committee of the Whole by unanimous consent, typically after having passed through more than one stage of the legislative process in a single sitting. The House may also adopt a special order to refer a bill to a Committee of the Whole.[99]

Most bills are referred to the standing committee whose "mandate most closely corresponds to the bill's subject matter." However, the House may consider referring a bill to a legislative committee, "a distinct type of committee created solely to undertake the consideration of legislation."[100]

4. Reporting and Third Reading

During the reporting stage the committee submits its report, which may recommend that the bill be accepted as it was in its first reading, or with amendments, or that it not be advanced further. During report stage debate, members, "particularly those who were not members of the committee,"[101] can propose further amendments to the bill. Written notice is necessary and discussion of the bill "focuses on the amendments and not on the bill as a whole."[102]

According to the *Compendium*, if no amendments are proposed during the reporting stage and the bill is adopted as is, then there is no debate and ". . . it may go immediately to third reading for adoption. A bill that has been reported by a Committee of the Whole, with or without amendment, must be put to a vote immediately at report stage and may proceed to third reading the same day."[103]

---

[96] Standing Orders of the House of Commons, Standing Order 71(1)–(2).

[97] *Stages in the Legislative Process, supra* note 91.

[98] *Legislative Process, supra* note 73.

[99] *Stages in the Legislative Process, supra* note 91.

[100] *Legislative Process, supra* note 73.

[101] *Id.*

[102] *Id.*

[103] *Id.*; *See also* Standing Orders of the House of Commons, Standing Order 76.1(11).

The third reading is regarded as the final stage through which a bill must pass in the House of Commons and "debate at this stage of the legislative process focuses on the final form of the bill."[104] It is a stage where Members must determine whether the bill should be adopted by the House.[105] When the motion for third reading has carried, the Clerk of the House certifies that the bill has passed[106] and the Bill is then sent to the Senate for approval. Defeat of a motion for third reading will result in the withdrawal of the bill.[107]

5. Repeated in Other House

The legislative process of the Senate is very similar to the one in the House of Commons, described above.[108] However, it should be noted that the Senate cannot "initiate money bills (i.e. bills imposing taxes or providing for the collection or spending of public money)."[109] The Senate Fact Sheet summarizes the relationship between the Senate and House of Commons in the legislative process as follows:

> If the bill was introduced in the Senate, it is sent to the House of Commons, which will examine it in a similar three-reading process. If the bill was introduced in the House of Commons and *was not* amended in the Senate, it is now ready for Royal Assent.
>
> If a bill introduced [sic] in the House of Commons and was amended in the Senate, a message about the amendments is sent to the Commons, asking for their agreement. If the Senate and the House of Commons do not agree on the contents of a bill, they may propose amendments until they reach agreement. Once the two Houses agree on a final version, the bill is granted Royal Assent by the Queen or one of her Canadian representatives (usually the Governor General or a deputy), making it law.[110]

6. Royal Assent

Royal Assent is a process by which a representative of the Crown approves an identical bill to one that has been passed by both houses of Parliament. According to a Senate Procedural Note,

> [t]he legislative process by which a bill becomes part of the law of the land requires the participation and approval of the three components of Parliament: the Crown, the Senate and the House of Commons. Royal Assent and the accompanying ceremony, where all

---

[104] *Id.*

[105] *Id.*

[106] Standing Orders of the House of Commons, Standing Order 72.

[107] *Legislative Process, supra* note 73.

[108] *Id.*

[109] *Senate of Canada Fact Sheet: The Senate and Legislation*, PARLIAMENT OF CANADA, http://sen.parl.gc.ca/portal/publications/factsheets/fs-legislation-e htm, *archived at* https://perma.cc/K9P6-YASF.

[110] *Id.*

three institutions are present, are the visible manifestation of the Crown sanctioning the work of Parliament.[111]

Royal Assent is the last stage that a bill must complete before officially becoming an Act of Parliament and part of Canada's laws. Royal Assent can be given by "the Governor General or either a Justice of the Supreme Court of Canada or the Secretary to the Governor General, acting as deputy of the Governor General."[112] Royal Assent may be given in two ways: by ceremony, or by written declaration. If it is conveyed through a ceremony, "Royal Assent is accorded in the Senate Chamber in the presence of members of the House and Senate."[113] Prior to the passage of the Royal Assent Act of 2002,[114] this was the only means to signify approval, but since 2002 it may be signified by a written declaration.[115]

---

[111] *Senate Procedural Notes No. 6, Royal Assent*, PARLIAMENT OF CANADA (Sept. 2012), http://www.parl.gc.ca/About/senate/proceduralNotes/pdf/Procedural-Note-6.pdf, *archived at* https://perma.cc/K74C-CU5N.

[112] *Id.*

[113] *Royal Assent*, THE GOVERNOR GENERAL OF CANADA, http://www.gg.ca/document.aspx?id=13989 (last updated Dec. 14, 2010), *archived at* https://perma.cc/K83H-2BRQ.

[114] Royal Assent Act S.C. 2002, c. 15, § 2, http://laws-lois.justice.gc.ca/eng/acts/R-8.6/page-1.html, *archived at* https://perma.cc/64C6-2SG6.

[115] *Id.*

People's Republic of China

Laney Zhang
Senior Foreign Law Specialist

SUMMARY   The National People's Congress (NPC) of the People's Republic of China is the highest organ of state power under the Constitution. The Constitution grants the NPC and its Standing Committee legislative power, decisional power, supervisory power, and power of appointment and removal. The NPC convenes once a year, while the Standing Committee usually convenes once every other month.

Each plenary session of the NPC elects a Presidium for that session, which presides over the NPC plenary sessions and is deemed the "omnipotent center of power in the NPC." The NPC deputies are grouped into delegations based on the units that elect them. The Law Committee deliberates on all bills submitted to the NPC and the NPC Standing Committee, and other Special Committees are also responsible for commenting on legislation in their specific policy areas.

In the NPC legislative process, the NPC Presidium and specified state actors may propose bills to an NPC session. An individual deputy to the NPC cannot propose a bill in his or her own capacity. In theory a delegation or a group of thirty or more deputies may introduce a bill; however, most of these measures do not make their way to the agenda of the NPC session. A bill is passed by a majority vote in the NPC.

In the Standing Committee legislative process, the Council of Chairmen and specified state actors may propose bills to the Standing Committee session. Ten or more members of the Standing Committee may jointly propose a bill, but it is up to the Council of Chairmen whether or not to place it on the agenda of the Standing Committee session. Bills are generally deliberated three times in the Standing Committee before being put to a vote.

After a bill is passed in the NPC or NPC Standing Committee, it is signed by the President of the State and promulgated by an Order of the President.

I. Background

The National People's Congress (NPC) of the People's Republic of China (PRC or China) was officially established on September 15, 1954, when the first session of the first NPC was held.[1] PRC's first formal Constitution, namely the 1954 Constitution, was passed by the first NPC.[2]

Three NPCs convened before 1966, when the Great Cultural Revolution was launched. During the following ten years, the NPC was effectively shut down.[3] In 1975, just before the end of the

---

[1] *About Congress: Introduction of the System of People's Congress*, THE NATIONAL PEOPLE'S CONGRESS OF THE PEOPLE'S REPUBLIC OF CHINA (Dec. 7, 2015), http://www.npc.gov.cn/englishnpc/about/2007-11/20/content_1373250.htm, *archived at* https://perma.cc/US2D-4XJL.

[2] ZHANG QIANFAN, THE CONSTITUTION OF CHINA: A CONTEXTUAL ANALYSIS 44 (2012).

Cultural Revolution, the NPC reconvened and managed to pass the 1975 Constitution. In 1978 the NPC enacted a third Constitution, which was replaced by the current Constitution enacted by the fifth session of the fifth NPC in 1982. The 1982 Constitution was amended by each NPC from the seventh to tenth, respectively, in 1988, 1993, 1999, and 2004.[4]

The period between the drafting of the 1982 Constitution and the enactment of the Law on Legislation in 2000 is deemed a reform era of the NPC.[5] The NPC developed on the basis of the 1982 Constitution is a unique institution compared to other parliaments around the world, in terms of its constitutional status, the role of its Standing Committee, its large deputy body, its legislative processes, etc.

The NPC sessions have been held in the Great Hall of the People since the Hall was built in 1959. The Hall is located on the west side of Tiananmen Square in Beijing.[6]

II. Constitutional Status and Role

A. Highest Organ of State Power

Article 57 of the Constitution declares that the NPC is the highest organ of state power.[7] Such a status is "implied in the unitary constitutional structure, where the highest power is singularly lodged in the central (national) government and its laws and regulations enjoy unlimited supremacy."[8] Meanwhile, China's unitary framework accommodates institutional compromises such as the regional autonomy of ethnic minorities and special administrative regions of Hong Kong and Macao.[9]

All power in the PRC belongs to the people, as stated the Constitution.[10] The NPC and local people's congresses (LPCs) are designed by the Constitution to have supreme authority so that the people may rule the country that belongs to them.[11] According to the Constitution, the people exercise state power through the NPC and LPCs, which are constituted through democratic elections. They are responsible to the people and subject to their supervision. The

---

[3] JIANG JINSONG, THE NATIONAL PEOPLE'S CONGRESS OF CHINA 60–61 (2003).

[4] ZHANG, *supra* note 2, at 46–47; XIANFA [CONSTITUTION] art. 57 (1982), 2004 FAGUI HUIBIAN 4–28.

[5] JIANG, *supra* note 3, at 76.

[6] *Renmin Dahuitang Jiancheng* [*Construction of the Great Hall of the People*], DANGSHI BAI KE, http://dangshi. people.com.cn/GB/165617/166495/168115/10002879.html (last visited Dec. 14, 2015), *archived at* https://perma.cc/9XNF-HMDS.

[7] CONSTITUTION art. 57.

[8] ZHANG, *supra* note 2, at 124.

[9] *Id.* at 108–15.

[10] CONSTITUTION art. 2.

[11] ZHANG, *supra* note 2, at 121.

administrative, judicial, and procuratorial organs of the state are created by the people's congresses to which they are responsible and by which they are supervised.[12]

Nevertheless, commentators state that, in practice, the NPC's supreme status may have largely been reduced to endorsing decisions made by the Chinese Communist Party (CCP), whose leadership is also explicitly recognized by the Constitution.[13]

B. Constitutional Powers of the NPC

The powers of the NPC are mainly set out in article 62 of the Constitution. Its powers are generally categorized into four major types: legislative power, power to make decisions regarding major national political issues, supervisory power, and the power of appointment and removal.[14]

1. Legislative Power

According the Constitution, the NPC has the power to

- amend the Constitution;[15] and

- enact and amend basic laws, which includes laws governing criminal offenses, civil affairs, state organs, and "other basic laws."[16]

2. Decisional Power

The decisional power granted to the NPC by the Constitution includes the power to

- examine and approve the plan for national economic and social development and the report on its implementation;[17]

- examine and approve the state budget and the report on its implementation;[18]

- alter or annul inappropriate decisions of the NPC Standing Committee;[19]

- approve the establishment of provinces, autonomous regions, and municipalities directly under the Central Government;[20]

---

[12] CONSTITUTION arts. 2 & 3.

[13] ZHANG, *supra* note 2, at 122; CONSTITUTION pmbl.

[14] *Id.*; ZHANG, *supra* note 2, at 127–29.

[15] CONSTITUTION art. 62, § 1.

[16] *Id.* art. 62, § 3.

[17] *Id.* art. 62, § 9.

[18] *Id.* art. 62, § 10.

[19] *Id.* art. 62, § 11.

[20] *Id.* art. 62, § 12.

- decide on the establishment of special administrative regions and the systems to be instituted there;[21] and

- decide on questions of war and peace.[22]

3. Supervisory Power

Under the Constitution, the NPC supervises the enforcement of the Constitution.[23] In addition, the State Council is responsible to and reports its work to the NPC.[24] The Supreme People's Court (SPC) and the Supreme People's Procuratorate (SPP) are responsible to the NPC and its Standing Committee.[25] The NPC and the NPC Standing Committee can question the State Council and its ministries and commissions.[26]

4. Power of Appointment and Removal

A unique characteristic of the Chinese NPC is that it not only elects top-ranking state officials, but also elects key officials of the judicial branch.[27] According to the Constitution, the NPC can

- elect the President and the Vice-President of the State;[28]

- decide on the choice of the Premier of the State Council upon nomination by the President, and on the choice of the Vice-Premiers, State Councilors, Ministers in charge of ministries or commissions, Auditor-General, and Secretary-General of the State Council upon nomination by the Premier;[29]

- elect the Chairman of the Central Military Commission (CMC) and, upon nomination by the Chairman, decide on the choice of all other members of the CMC;[30]

- elect the President of the SPC;[31]

- elect the Procurator-General of the SPP;[32] and

- remove from office the above personnel.[33]

---

[21] *Id.* art. 62, § 13.

[22] *Id.* art. 62, § 14.

[23] *Id.* art. 62, § 2.

[24] *Id.* art. 92.

[25] *Id.* arts. 128 & 133.

[26] *Id.* art. 73.

[27] ZHANG, *supra* note 2, at 127.

[28] CONSTITUTION art. 62, § 4.

[29] *Id.* art. 62, § 5.

[30] *Id.* art. 62, § 6.

[31] *Id.* art. 62, § 7.

[32] *Id.* art. 62, § 8.

In addition, the Constitution supplements the powers granted to the NPC with an open-ended authorization that gives the NPC the authority to exercise "other functions and powers as the highest organ of state power should exercise."[34]

III. Structure and Composition

China's NPC is unicameral, with laws only needing to pass one chamber to take effect. The NPC Standing Committee is sometimes seen as, in essence, a "second chamber" enjoying independent legislative authority, but not in the same sense as in bicameralism, which usually requires a bill to receive a majority vote in both chambers in order to become law.[35]

The current twelfth NPC has 2,987 deputies in total.[36] According to the Election Law of the NPC and LPCs, the total number of deputies of the NPC shall not exceed three thousand.[37]

Pursuant to the Constitution, the NPC meets only once a year.[38] It normally meets in March for about ten days. Although the Constitution provides that the NPC may hold interim sessions whenever the Standing Committee deems it necessary, in practice no such session has ever taken place.[39]

A. NPC Standing Committee

The permanent body of the NPC, the NPC Standing Committee, usually convenes once every other month.[40] The current twelfth NPC Standing Committee has 161 members.[41] It is a unique characteristic of the Chinese NPC system that the Standing Committee is granted independent legislative power by the Constitution, as well other powers of the state, some of which are even not ordinarily available to the NPC.[42]

---

[33] *Id.* art. 63.

[34] *Id.* art. 62, § 15.

[35] ZHANG, *supra* note 2, at 53, 132.

[36] *Lijie Quanguo Renda Lici Huiyi* [*Sessions of NPCs*], XINHUANET, http://news.xinhuanet.com/ziliao/2003-01/18/content_695280.htm (last visited Dec. 14, 2015), *archived at* https://perma.cc/T489-PWFZ.

[37] Quanguo Renmin Daibiao Dahui he Difang Geji Renmin Daibiao Dahui Xuanju Fa [Election Law of the National People's Congress and Local People's Congresses] (promulgated by the NPC, July 1, 1979, last rev. Aug. 29, 2015) art. 15, http://www.gov.cn/zhengce/2015-08/30/content_2922358.htm, *archived at* https://perma.cc/39LM-9NCE (Election Law).

[38] CONSTITUTION art. 61.

[39] ZHANG, *supra* note 2, at 125.

[40] Election Law art. 29.

[41] Shi'er Jie Quanguo Renda Changweihui Weiyuan Mingdan (161 Ren) [Name List of the 12th NPC Standing Committee (161 Members)], XINHUANET (Mar. 14, 2013), *available at* http://news.ifeng.com/mainland/special/2013lianghui/detail_2013_03/14/23114200_0.shtml, *archived at* https://perma.cc/N2EZ-MCJ5.

[42] ZHANG, *supra* note 2, at 135.

1. Constitutional Powers of the NPC Standing Committee

According to the Constitution, the NPC Standing Committee can

- interpret the Constitution;[43]

- enact and amend laws other than those that must be enacted by the NPC;[44]

- partially supplement and amend laws enacted by the NPC when the NPC is not in session, as long as "the basic principles of these laws are not contravened;"[45] and

- interpret laws.[46]

In addition to the legislative power, numerous other state powers are also specifically granted to the NPC Standing Committee by the Constitution, including decisional power, supervisory power, and the power of appointment and removal.[47] Under the category of supervisory power, for example, the Standing Committee can

- supervise enforcement of the Constitution;[48]

- annul administrative regulations, decisions, or orders of the State Council that contravene the Constitution or other laws;[49] and

- annul local regulations or decisions of the organs of state power of provinces, autonomous regions, and municipalities directly under the Central Government that contravene the Constitution, other laws, or administrative regulations.[50]

2. Leadership Roles

The NPC Standing Committee is composed of the Chairman, Vice-Chairmen, Secretary-General, and other members.[51] The Chairman of the Standing Committee of the NPC directs the work of the Standing Committee and convenes its sessions. The Vice-Chairmen and the Secretary-

---

[43] CONSTITUTION art. 67, § 1.

[44] *Id.* art. 67, § 2.

[45] *Id.* art. 67, § 3.

[46] *Id.* art. 67, § 4.

[47] JIANG, *supra* note 3, at 150.

[48] CONSTITUTION art. 67, § 1.

[49] *Id.* art. 67, § 7.

[50] *Id.* art. 67, § 8.

[51] *Id.* art. 65.

General assist with the Chairman's work.[52] The current twelfth NPC Standing Committee has a total of thirteen Vice-Chairmen.[53]

The Chairman, Vice-Chairmen, and Secretary-General constitute the Council of Chairmen, which handles important day-to-day work of the NPC Standing Committee.[54] According to the NPC Organic Law, the Council of Chairmen can

- decide on the time for each session of the Standing Committee and draft the agenda of the session;

- decide whether the bills, proposals, and questions submitted to the Standing Committee should be referred to the relevant Special Committees or submitted to the plenary session of the Standing Committee for deliberation;

- direct and coordinate the daily work of the Special Committees; and

- carry out other important daily work of the Standing Committee.[55]

3. Administrative Bodies

The daily work of the NPC Standing Committee is supported by a number of administrative bodies, including the General Office, the Legislative Affairs Commission, the Budgetary Affairs Commission, the Hong Kong Special Administrative Region Basic Law Committee, and the Macao Special Administrative Region Basic Law Committee.[56] Being composed of professional staff, most of whom are neither Standing Committee members nor NPC deputies, the Legislative Affairs Commission is in charge of daily lawmaking and review activities.[57]

B. Presidium

Each plenary session of the NPC begins with a preparatory meeting, in which a Presidium and a Secretary-General for that session are elected.[58] The Presidium presides over the NPC sessions.[59]

---

[52] *Id.* art. 68.

[53] *Di Shi'er Jie Quanguo Renmin Daibiao Dahui Changwu Weiyuanhui [Standing Committee of the Twelfth NPC]*, THE CENTRAL PEOPLE'S GOVERNMENT OF THE PEOPLE'S REPUBLIC OF CHINA (Mar. 14, 2013), http://www.gov.cn/test/2013-03/14/content_2353702.htm, *archived at* https://perma.cc/WLE4-2WG5.

[54] *Id.*

[55] Quanguo Renmin Daibiao Dahui Zuzhi Fa [NPC Organic Law] (Organic Law) (promulgated by the NPC, Dec. 20, 1982) art. 25, 1982 FAGUI HUIBIAN 68–79.

[56] *Renda Jigou [Organs of the NPC]*, http://www.npc.gov.cn/npc/rdjg/node_507.htm (last visited Dec. 14, 2015), *archived at* https://perma.cc/QY7Z-KDCF.

[57] ZHANG, *supra* note 2, at 138.

[58] Organic Law art. 5.

[59] *Id.* art. 6.

The Presidium is deemed the "omnipotent center of power in the NPC,"[60] and is sometimes viewed as a platform through which the CCP controls the NPC, particularly given that it is composed of leading Party and state leaders.[61] A Presidium is typically composed of: (1) major leaders of the CCP and the state; (2) members of the CMC; (3) chairs of the "democratic parties;" (4) persons in charge of central party, state, and military organs; (5) persons in charge of officially recognized "people's organizations;" and (6) heads of the delegations.[62]

C. Delegations

The NPC deputies are grouped into delegations based on the units that elect them.[63] Each delegation elects a head and deputy heads. Before each session of the NPC is convened, the delegations discuss matters concerning preparations for the session put forward by the NPC Standing Committee. During the session, the delegations "deliberate on the bills and proposals submitted to the Congress," and the delegation heads or representatives may express opinions on the bills and proposals at either the Presidium meetings or the plenary meetings of the session.[64]

D. Special Committees

The NPC establishes special committees that are subject to the leadership of the NPC, and to the NPC Standing Committee when the NPC is not in session.[65] The committees are composed of deputies who specialize in the committee's policy area.[66] The Law Committee deliberates on all bills submitted to the NPC and the NPC Standing Committee, and other special committees are also responsible for commenting on legislation in their specific policy areas.[67]

Currently, there are a total of nine special committees in the NPC: the Nationalities Committee; the Law Committee; the Judicial Committee of Internal Affairs; the Finance and Economic Committee; the Education, Science, Culture, and Public Health Committee; the Foreign Affairs Committee; the Overseas Chinese Committee; the Environmental and Resource Protection Committee; and the Agricultural and Rural Committee.[68]

The special committees are usually headed by a Vice-Chairman of the NPC Standing Committee, and the Standing Committee members constitute the majority on the special committees.[69]

---

[60] JIANG, *supra* note 3, at 159.

[61] ZHANG, *supra* note 2, at 126.

[62] *Id.*

[63] Organic Law art. 4.

[64] *Id.*

[65] *Id.* art. 35.

[66] ZHANG, *supra* note 2, at 126.

[67] Organic Law art. 37.

[68] *Renda Jigou, supra* note 56.

[69] ZHANG, *supra* note 2, at 126–27.

E. Political Parties

In addition to the ruling CCP, in China there are officially eight "democratic parties" supporting the CCP, each having members seated in the NPC and the NPC Standing Committee. In the NPC and the NPC Standing Committee, however, members of the democratic parties are not organized and do not act in the name of their parties.

The democratic parties are as follows:

- Revolutionary Committee of the China Kuomingtang

- China Democratic League

- China Democratic National Construction Association

- China Association for Promoting Democracy

- Chinese Peasants' and Workers' Democratic Party

- China Zhi Gong Dang of China

- Jiusan Society

- Taiwan Democratic Self-Government League[70]

IV. Elections

The NPC and the NPC Standing Committee are elected for a term of five years.[71] The Standing Committee is obligated to complete the election of deputies of the succeeding NPC two months prior to the expiration of the term of office of the current NPC.[72] The term of the current twelfth NPC is from March 2013 to March 2018.[73]

Ordinary deputies may run for consecutive terms,[74] while the Chairman and Vice-Chairmen of the Standing Committee may serve no more than two consecutive terms.[75]

According to the Constitution, deputies of the NPC are elected from the provinces, autonomous regions, municipalities directly under the Central Government, special administrative regions, and armed forces.[76] Specifically, deputies of the NPC are elected by deputies of the provincial congresses, which in turn are elected by city- or county-level deputies.[77] Deputies to the

---

[70] JIANG, *supra* note 3, at 308–31.

[71] CONSTITUTION art. 60.

[72] *Id.*

[73] *Lijie Quanguo Renda Lici Huiyi, supra* note 36.

[74] ZHANG, *supra* note 2, at 125.

[75] CONSTITUTION art. 66.

[76] *Id.* art. 59.

[77] Election Law art. 2.

people's congresses of cities not divided into districts, municipal districts, counties, autonomous counties, townships, nationality townships, and towns are directly elected.[78]

V. Legislative Process

A. Legislative Process in the NPC

1. Proposing Bills

The NPC Presidium may initiate the legislative process by proposing bills to the NPC.[79] Many state actors are also authorized to propose bills, which are to be placed on the agenda of the NPC session by the Presidium. The state actors include the NPC Standing Committee, State Council, CMC, SPC, SPP, and the NPC Special Committees.[80]

An individual deputy to the NPC cannot propose a bill in his or her own capacity. Although in theory a delegation or a group of thirty or more deputies may introduce a bill, it is up to the Presidium whether or not to place the bill on the agenda of the NPC session. The Presidium may refer such a bill to the relevant special committee for deliberation and comments.[81] Most bills proposed by ordinary deputies do not pass the special committee deliberation in order to make their way to the agenda.[82]

2. Deliberation

The NPC plenary session hears the statements of the bill sponsor of a proposed bill that has been placed on the agenda of the current NPC session.[83] The delegations then deliberate on the bill.[84] The bill is also subject to deliberation by the relevant special committee.[85] Based on the deliberated opinions of the delegations and the special committee, the Law Committee considers the bill and submits to the Presidium a report on the result of its deliberations containing different opinions and a revised draft law.[86]

---

[78] *Id.*

[79] Li Fa Fa [Law on Legislation] (promulgated by National People's Congress (NPC), Mar. 15, 2000, rev. Mar. 15, 2015) art. 14, http://news.xinhuanet.com/politics/2015lh/2015-03/18/c_1114682142.htm, *archived at* https://perma.cc/XME7-UCVT.

[80] Law on Legislation art. 14.

[81] *Id.* art. 15.

[82] ZHANG, *supra* note 2, at 130.

[83] Law on Legislation art. 18.

[84] *Id.*

[85] *Id.* art. 19.

[86] *Id.* art. 20.

3. Voting

After a revised draft law has been considered by the delegations, the Law Committee further revises the draft according to the deliberated opinions of the delegations and prepares a draft for vote. The Presidium then submits the draft to the plenary session for a vote. A bill passes by a majority vote in the NPC.[87]

4. Promulgation

After a law is passed in the NPC, it is signed by the President of the State and promulgated by an Order of the President.[88] The President does not have a veto or discretion in signing once the law has been passed by the NPC.[89]

B. Legislative Process in the NPC Standing Committee

1. Proposing Bills

The Council of Chairmen may propose bills to a meeting of the Standing Committee for deliberation. State actors, including the State Council, CMC, SPC, SPP, and special committees of the NPC, may also propose bills, which are to be placed on the agenda of the current Standing Committee session by the Council of Chairmen. The Council of Chairmen may also forward a bill to the relevant special committee for deliberation and comments before placing it on the agenda.[90]

Ten or more members of the Standing Committee may jointly propose a bill, but it is up to the Council of Chairmen whether or not to place it on the agenda of the current Standing Committee session, with or without forwarding it to a special committee for deliberation and comments.[91] The Council of Chairmen is required by law either to report to the Standing Committee or to explain to the sponsor why it has decided not to place the bill on the agenda.[92]

2. Deliberation

Any proposed bill placed on the agenda of the Standing Committee session is generally deliberated three times in the Standing Committee before being put to a vote.[93] Bills for which "various parties concerned have formed a preponderant consensus" may be put to a vote after deliberations at two Standing Committee sessions, and may be put to vote even after only one

---

[87] *Id.* art. 24.

[88] *Id.*

[89] ZHANG, *supra* note 2, at 130.

[90] Law on Legislation art. 26.

[91] *Id.* art. 27.

[92] *Id.*

[93] *Id.* art. 29.

deliberation if the bill only seeks to regulate very specific matters or has only been partially revised.[94]

In the first deliberation, the statements of the bill sponsor are heard by the plenary session, and then the bill is preliminarily deliberated on in group meetings. In the second deliberation, the report of the Law Committee on the revision of the bill is heard by the plenary session before the bill is further deliberated on in group meetings. In the third deliberation, the report of the Law Committee on the result of deliberation of the bill is heard by the plenary session, and then the revised draft law is deliberated on in group meetings.[95]

The Law Committee is obligated to deliberate on the bill based on the deliberation opinions of the members of the Standing Committee and other relevant actors, issue a summary report on revisions or a deliberation conclusion report containing different opinions, and prepare the revised draft law.[96]

3. Publishing a Draft Law for Public Comment

According to a provision newly added to the Law on Legislation in March 2015, for all bills on the agenda of Standing Committee sessions, the draft law and explanation on its drafting and revision must be published for public comment, unless the Council of Chairmen decides otherwise.[97]

4. Voting

After the revised draft of a law has been deliberated by the Standing Committee session, the Law Committee further revises it on the basis of the deliberated opinions of the members of the Standing Committee and prepares the draft for a vote. A bill is passed by a majority vote in the Standing Committee.[98]

5. Promulgation

After a bill is passed in the NPC Standing Committee, it is signed by the President of the State and promulgated by an Order of the President.[99]

---

[94] *Id.* art. 30.

[95] *Id.* art. 29.

[96] *Id.* art. 33.

[97] *Id.* art. 37.

[98] *Id.* art. 41.

[99] *Id.* art. 44.

Finland

Elin Hofverberg
Foreign Law Research Consultant

SUMMARY   Finland is a parliamentary republic. The Parliament is unicameral with two hundred members representing thirteen geographic areas and belonging to eight different parties. Bills are passed by a simple majority. There are special rules for the adoption of the budget bill as well as amendments to the Constitution. Bills are initiated by the government or members of Parliament and are considered by committees and debated in the Parliament.

I. Background

Finland is a republic with a unicameral Parliament.[1] The Finnish Parliament is bilingual—all work must be conducted in both Finnish and Swedish, and all material that requires a vote must be published in both Finnish and Swedish.[2] Sessions of Parliament start on February 1 of each year.[3]

A. Creation of Parliament

The Finnish Parliament[4] first held regular meetings in 1863, while Finland was still part of the Russian Empire.[5] However, even while part of Sweden during the eighteenth century, Finland had a representative body similar to a parliament.

The Finnish Parliament declared itself as the highest organ of legislative power (supreme organ of State) weeks before Finland formally became independent from Russia in 1917.[6] In 1919 the Finnish Constitution was established, which gave the Finnish Parliament power to legislate and make decisions regarding the country's finances.[7]

---

[1] 1 and 2 §§ FINLANDS GRUNDLAG [FINNISH CONSTITUTION] (FINLANDS FÖRFATTNINGSSAMLING [FFS] 11.6.1999/731), http://www.finlex.fi/sv/laki/ajantasa/1999/19990731?search[type]=pika&search[pika]=grundlag (in Swedish), *archived at* http://perma.cc/L8GS-MK8V, *and* http://www.finlex.fi/fi/laki/ajantasa/1999/19990731 (in Finnish), *archived at* http://perma.cc/X7XA-GH75.

[2] 51 § CONSTITUTION.

[3] 1 § RIKSDAGENS ARBETSORDNING [PARLIAMENTARY WORKING ORDER](FFS 17.12.1999/40 år 2000), http://www.finlex.fi/sv/laki/ajantasa/2000/ 20000040, *archived at* http://perma.cc/QP8D-ZBX9.

[4] *Edeskunta* in Finnish, *Riksdag* in Swedish.

[5] *Brief History of Parliament – From Autonomy to EU Finland*, EDUSKUNTA/RIKSDAGEN, https://www.eduskunta.fi/EN/tietoaeduskunnasta/historia/Pages/default.aspx (last visited Dec. 4, 2015), *archived at* https://perma.cc/S4QS-8WPN.

[6] *Id.*

[7] 3 § CONSTITUTION.

B. The Edeskunta Building

The building in which the Parliament meets is located in Helsinki (the Finnish capital) and has served as the parliamentary building since 1931.[8] Prior to 1931, the Parliament met in the Heimola building, a building that was torn down in the 1960s.[9] Finland's Parliament Building is currently undergoing renovation ahead of the centennial of Finland's independence, which will be celebrated in 2017.[10] While the Parliament Building is undergoing renovation, the Parliament convenes at the adjacent Sibelius Academy building.[11]

C. Political Rights Highlights

The Finnish Parliament was the first parliament in the world to welcome female elected members, which occurred during the 1907 session, after women gained both the right to vote and run for office in 1906.[12]

II. Constitutional Status and Role

Finland is a sovereign parliamentary republic.[13] As such, Finland has both a President and a Prime Minister. Parliament represents the people, legislates, and determines the state's finances.[14]

The Constitution guarantees the municipalities a degree of independence by establishing that the governance of municipalities should be based on the principle of self-governance by its inhabitants.[15] The powers and responsibilities of the municipalities are governed by the Municipalities Act.[16] The municipalities are responsible for providing basic services to their inhabitants, such as health care and social services.[17]

---

[8] PARLIAMENT OF FINLAND, DEMOCRACY'S LONG ROAD: FINLAND'S REPRESENTATIVE DEMOCRACY AND CIVIL SOCIETY FROM 1863 TO THE PRESENT DAY 13 (May 2013), https://www.eduskunta.fi/FI/tietoaeduskunnasta/ esitemateriaalit/Documents/2013_Eduskunta_1863_Kansanvallan_pitka_tie_ENG_LORES300413[1].pdf, *archived at* https://perma.cc/UEH5-E92F.

[9] EDESKUNTA, PARLIAMENT OF FINLAND 22 (2012), https://www.eduskunta.fi/FI/tietoaeduskunnasta/esitemateriaalit/ Documents/2012Eduskunta_Yleisesite_ENG_LORES.pdf, *archived at* https://perma.cc/DDX8-2EH5.

[10] *Id.* at 23.

[11] *Renovation of Parliament's Properties*, EDESKUNTA/RIKSDAGEN, https://www.eduskunta.fi/EN/tietoaedus kunnasta/peruskorjaus/Pages/default.aspx (last visited Nov. 16, 2015), *archived at* https://perma.cc/RZ9X-4UPV.

[12] *Centenary of Women's Full Political Rights in Finland*, HELSINKI.FI, http://www.helsinki.fi/sukupuolentutkimus/ aanioikeus/en (last visited Dec. 14, 2015), *archived at* http://perma.cc/LCB6-QSQM.

[13] 1:1 § CONSTITUTION.

[14] *Id.* 1:3 §.

[15] *Id.* 121 §.

[16] KOMMUNALLAG, 10.4.2015/410, http://www.finlex.fi/sv/laki/ajantasa/2015/20150410?search[type]=pika&search [pika]=10.4.2015%2F410, *archived at* http://perma.cc/EW6V-F895.

[17] *Kommunerna och kommunalförvaltning*, SUOMI.fi, http://www.suomi.fi/suomifi/svenska/staten_och_ kommunerna/kommunerna_och_kommunalforvaltning/index.html?sort=2 (last visited Dec. 3, 2015), *archived at* http://perma.cc/5HH8-XAMQ.

III. Structure and Composition

A. General

The Finnish Parliament is unicameral and has two hundred members who sit for four-year terms.[18] Members of Parliament (MPs) are elected through direct, proportional, secret ballot elections.[19] All votes carry the same weight.[20]

There are currently eight parties in the Finnish Parliament:[21] the Center Party[22] (21.1% of the national vote and forty-nine seats); the National Coalitions Party[23] (18.1%, thirty-seven seats); the Finns Party[24] (17.6%, thirty-eight seats); the Social Democratic Party of Finland[25] (16.5%, thirty-four seats); the Greens[26] (8.5%, fifteen seats); the Left Alliance[27] (7.1%, twelve seats); the Swedish People's Party of Finland[28] (4.9%, nine seats); and the Christian Democrats of Finland[29] (3.5%, five seats).

B. Speaker

At each session of Parliament there is one Speaker[30] and two Vice-speakers,[31] who are elected by the Parliament.[32] The Speaker of the Finnish Parliament has the role of opening Parliament.

The responsibilities of the speakership are prescribed in law (Riksdagens arbetsordning).[33] They include overseeing the work of the Parliament as well as it internal governance, suggesting

---

[18] 24 § CONSTITUTION.

[19] *Id.* 25 §.

[20] *Id.*

[21] *Centern i Finland segrade i riksdagsvalet 2015*, STATISTIKCENTRALEN FINLAND (Apr. 30, 2015), http://www.stat.fi/til/evaa/2015/evaa_2015_2015-04-21_tie_001_sv.html, *archived at* http://perma.cc/M5C8-RS8Q.

[22] KESKUSTA, http://www.keskusta.fi/ (last visited Dec. 3, 2015), *archived at* http://perma.cc/Y66F-MQS2.

[23] KOKOOMUS, https://www.kokoomus.fi/en/ (last visited Dec. 3, 2015), *archived at* https://perma.cc/6M7K-GAKF.

[24] PERUS, http://www.perussuomalaiset.fi (last visited Dec. 3, 2015), *archived at* http://perma.cc/9EBW-XL69.

[25] SDP, http://www.sdp.fi (last visited Dec. 3, 2015), *archived at* http://perma.cc/7M6T-LP2E.

[26] *Welcome!*, VIHREAT, https://www.vihreat.fi/vihreat-de-grona-greens-finland (last visited Dec. 3, 2015), *archived at* https://perma.cc/8YDR-ZMZ4 (click "Screen capture").

[27] VASEMMISTO, http://www.vasemmisto.fi (last visited Dec. 3, 2015), *archived at* http://perma.cc/2A8L-5MB8.

[28] SFP, http://www.sfp.fi (last visited Dec. 3, 2015), *archived at* http://perma.cc/54B4-N33V.

[29] KRISTILLISDEMOKRAATIT, http://www.kd.fi/english (last visited Dec. 3, 2015), *archived at* http://perma.cc/GZG2-9KC4.

[30] *Riksdagens arbete leds av presidiet*, EDESKUNTA/RIKSDAGEN, https://www.eduskunta.fi/SV/kansanedustajat/puhemies/Sidor/default.aspx (in Swedish; last visited Dec. 14, 2015), *archived at* http://perma.cc/FWB9-ZSSH.

[31] 34 § CONSTITUTION.

[32] 4 § RIKSDAGENS ARBETSORDNING.

[33] *Id.* 6 §.

which committee should deal with which bill and when a bill should be presented and voted on, deciding on the involvement of MPs in international cooperation, and other tasks that relate to the functioning of Parliament. [34] The Speaker does not participate in debates or votes in Parliament. [35]

C. Committees

There are fifteen permanent committees and an EU Commitee in Parliament. [36] In the Constitution the following five are specifically mentioned: the Grand Commitee (twenty-five members), the Constitutional Law Commitee (seventeen members), the Foreign Affairs Committee (seventeen members), the Finance Committee (seventeen members), and the Audit Committee. [37] The committees either have a specifically prescribed number of members, such as the Grand Committee, or eleven members if not specifically prescribed. [38]

The fifteen permanent committees are as follows:

- Grand Committee

- Constitutional Law Committee

- Foreign Affairs Committee

- Finance Committee

- Audit Committee

- Employment and Equality Committee

- Administration Committee

- Legal Affairs Committee

- Transport and Communications Committee

- Agriculture and Forestry Committee

- Defense Committee

- Education and Culture Committee

- Social Affairs and Health Committee

- Commerce Committee

---

[34] *Id.*

[35] 42 § CONSTITUTION.

[36] *Committees*, EDESKUNTA/RIKSDAGEN, https://www.eduskunta.fi/EN/lakiensaataminen/valiokunnat/Pages/default.aspx (last visited Dec. 14, 2015), *archived at* https://perma.cc/8ZSW-ERX3.

[37] 35 § CONSTITUTION.

[38] *Id.*

- Committee for the Future

- Environment Committee

Membership on a committee is based on the party's relative representation in Parliament.[39] Committees can make decisions when two-thirds of its members are present.[40] Committees must be constituted immediately after the Parliament has convened for its first session.[41] One of the committee's members is elected chairperson and acts as chairperson for the entirety of the mandate period.[42]

The work of the committees is regulated in the Parliamentary Working Order Act.[43]

D. Prime Minister

Parliament elects the Prime Minister, who is typically the leader of the party with the most seats in Parliament, after a nomination by the President.[44] There is no debate prior to the vote on Prime Minister.[45]

IV. Elections

A. General

Finland holds two separate elections—one for President and one to elect MPs. The date of the election for the Finnish Parliament is set in law as the third Sunday in April, every four years.[46] The next ordinary scheduled election for the Finnish Parliament is April 21, 2019.[47] There are no restrictions on how many terms an MP may serve.

Election for President is completely separate and by law is held on the fourth Sunday of January every six years.[48] A President may only serve two terms in succession.[49]

---

[39] *Committees*, EDESKUNTA/RIKSDAGEN, *supra* note 37.

[40] *Id.*

[41] 17 § RIKSDAGENS ARBETSORDNING.

[42] *Id.*

[43] *Id.* 7 §.

[44] *Id.* 65 §.

[45] *Id.*

[46] 107 § ELECTION Act.

[47] 54 § CONSTITUTION; 127 § VALLAG [ELECTION ACT] FFS 2.10.1998/714, https://www.finlex.fi/sv/laki/ajantasa/1998/19980714?search%5Btype%5D=pika&search%5Bpika%5D=vallag, *archived at* https://perma.cc/DN25-5ZUT.

[48] 54 § CONSTITUTION.

[49] *Id.*

B. Electoral Districts

The Constitution provides that Finland may have between twelve and eighteen electoral districts, not counting Åland,[50] which forms its own electoral district.[51] There is currently a total of thirteen electoral districts.[52]

The number of seats in each district is determined based on the number of Finnish citizens who are domiciled in the district as calculated on the last day of the sixth month preceding election day (generally October 31).[53] The number of Finnish citizens in the district are divided by the total number of citizens in the country, then multiplied by 199.[54] If a seat remains unclaimed following this calculation it will be given to the party with the largest decimal according to its result in the national election—i.e., a party with 4.9 votes will receive a seat prior to a party with 45.8 votes.[55]

C. Voter Turnout

Voter turnout has been consistently high in Finland. It was 70.7% in the first election with universal suffrage for men and women in 1907,[56] and 70.1% in the most recent election.[57]

D. Formation of Government

The leadership of the executive branch of government is constituted upon the election of a Prime Minister following a nomination by the President.[58] Ministers (Heads) of the government ministries are chosen by the Prime Minister, or if there is a coalition government through agreement between the coalition parties, prior to the formal election of Prime Minister.[59] Ministers do not need to be MPs.[60]

---

[50] Åland is a Swedish-speaking island in the Baltic Sea that has some autonomy in relation to Finland. For details see *Åland's Autonomy*, ALAND.AX, THE OFFICIAL ÅLAND WEBSITE (Aug. 26, 2013), http://www.aland.ax/en/fakta/sjalvstyrelsen, *archived at* https://perma.cc/9CPB-FQH8.

[51] 25 § CONSTITUTION

[52] 5 § ELECTION ACT.

[53] *Id.* 6 §.

[54] *Id.*

[55] *Id.*

[56] *Commitees*, EDESKUNTA/RIKSDAGEN, *supra* note 37.

[57] *Voter Turnout*, TULPOSPALVELU, http://tulospalvelu.vaalit.fi/E-2015/en/aanestys1.html (last visited Dec. 3, 2015), *archived at* https://perma.cc/28DJ-7QGN.

[58] 65 § RIKSDAGENS ARBETSORDNING.

[59] *Appointment and Organization*, FINNISH GOVERNMENT, http://valtioneuvosto.fi/en/government/appointment-and-organisation (last visited Jan. 11, 2016) *archived at* https://perma.cc/UYC8-JGFU.

[60] *Id.* (the only requirement is Finnish citizenship).

V. Legislative Process

The parliamentary legislative process is governed by the Riksdagens arbetsordning (Parliamentary Working Order).[61]

A. Ordinary Bills

Most of the legislative work is done in the ministries and committees.[62] Bills are initiated either through proposals by the government or by individual MPs.[63] Citizens' initiatives may also be brought forward, if backed by the signatures of at least 50,000 Finns.[64] After a proposal has been sent to the Central Office (Centralkansliet) in Parliament it must then be discussed by a committee, which can hears experts, before it is presented before Parliament.[65] Prior to a vote MPs may also debate the bill.[66]

The passage of a bill only requires a simple majority. If there are an equal number of votes for and against, a random drawing of yes and no votes is permitted and if the drawing is in favor of adopting the bill it will pass.[67]

B. Budget Bill

The budget bill is drafted and presented to the Parliament by the Government. The bill only requires a simple majority to pass. The budget expenses as well as the overarching appropriations are addressed in a separate regulation.[68]

After the Finance Committee has published its report the Government's budget bill is presented to Parliament *in plenum*.[69] Opposition parties or individual MPs may only present an alternative budget during a ten-day period after the Government's budget bill has been presented.[70] If Parliament does not approve the budget bill without changes, the Finance Committee continues its work and suggests changes to the bill. If a budget is not approved before the new fiscal year,

---

[61] 52 § CONSTITUTION.

[62] *See Legislative Drafting Process Guide*, FINLEX, http://lainvalmistelu.finlex.fi/en (last visited Dec. 3, 2015), *archived at* http://perma.cc/LP9R-WC33.

[63] 39 § CONSTITUTION.

[64] *Riksdagen stiftar lagar – så här blir en lag till*, EDESKUNTA/RIKSDAGEN, https://www.eduskunta.fi/SV/lakiensaataminen/lainvalmistelu_vaiheet/Sidor/default.aspx (last visited Dec. 3, 2015), *archived at* https://perma.cc/3XH8-5TA6.

[65] 40 § CONSTITUTION.

[66] 50 § RIKSDAGENS ARBETSORDNING.

[67] *Id.* 41 §.

[68] Förordning om statsbudgeten [Regulation on the State Budget] (FFS 11.12.1992/1243), http://www.finlex.fi/sv/laki/ajantasa/1992/19921243?search[type]=pika&search[pika]=budget, *archived at* http://perma.cc/LE8K-HBKH.

[69] 59 § RIKSDAGENS ARBETSORDNINGEN.

[70] *Id.* 20 §.

the Finance Committee must suggest how the budget proposal should temporarily be used as a governing budget.[71] Changes to the budget are adopted in the same manner as adoption of the budget itself.[72]

C. Changes to the Constitution

Changes to the Constitution require a two-thirds majority in two sessions, each held with a parliamentary election in between.[73]

---

[71] *Id.* 59 §.

[72] *Id.*

[73] 73 § CONSTITUTION.

France

Nicolas Boring
Foreign Law Specialist

SUMMARY   France is a unitary republic with a bicameral legislature composed of the National Assembly and the Senate.   The French constitutional system is often described as semipresidential, and is characterized by a structure of interconnecting powers between the legislative and executive branches.   The checks and balances between the legislative and executive branches include the President's power to dissolve the National Assembly, and the National Assembly's power to dismiss the Prime Minister, shared authority to initiate legislation between the Parliament and the Prime Minister, and the absence of any veto power on the part of the President.   The Parliament's powers are strictly enumerated by the Constitution, which lists the matters that can be the subject of legislation.

Members of the National Assembly are called deputies and are elected directly, in contrast with senators, who are chosen by indirect elections.   Deputies are elected for five-year terms.   Senators are elected for six-year terms, but elections are held every three years to elect an alternating half of the chamber.   Both chambers are organized in a similar manner, with a chamber president, a governing bureau, commissions, and formal political groups. Bills are submitted either by the Prime Minister or by members of either chamber.   Once submitted to one of the two chambers, a bill is first discussed, amended if need be, and voted on in commissions before being discussed, amended, and voted on by the chamber as a whole.   The bill must then go to the other chamber, where it follows the same procedure: discussion, possible amendment, and vote in commission followed by discussion, possible amendment, and vote in the chamber's plenary session.   A bill must be adopted by both chambers with identical language before it can be signed into law by the President of the Republic.   If the two chambers disagree on the terms of the bill, a joint commission comprised of seven deputies and seven senators is tasked with finding a compromise draft, although that compromise draft must still be voted on by both chambers.   In extreme cases of deadlock, the National Assembly may have the final say.

I. Background

The French Parliament was born in one of the opening acts of the French Revolution: on June 17, 1789, representatives of the Third Estate (i.e., commoners; the First Estate referred to the clergy and the Second Estate referred to the nobility) declared themselves to be the *Assemblée nationale* (National Assembly), and asserted themselves as the embodiment of national sovereignty and of the will of the French people.[1]   The constitutional history of France was tumultuous, however, and the names and forms of the French legislature changed many times, especially during the century following the Revolution.[2]   The French legislative branch ran the gamut from an elected

---

[1] *Histoire de l'Assemblée nationale* [*History of the National Assembly*], ASSEMBLEE-NATIONALE.FR (website of the National Assembly), http://www2.assemblee-nationale.fr/decouvrir-l-assemblee/histoire/histoire-de-l-assemblee-nationale#node_2027 (last visited Dec. 18, 2015), *archived at* https://perma.cc/43MS-CD2V.

[2] *Id.*

unicameral body (as in the Constitution of 1791), to an appointed tetracameral body (under Napoleon Bonaparte).[3] It was not until the Third Republic, shaped by the Constitutional Laws of 1875, that the notion of a democratically-elected bicameral legislature finally took root in an enduring manner. From then on, with the tragic exception of the Vichy Régime period (1940–1944), French legislative power always remained in the hands of an elected Parliament.[4]

The current constitutional system is known as the Fifth Republic, and is founded on the Constitution of October 4, 1958.[5] As described below, the Constitution gives crucial powers to Parliament, making it an institution of vital importance in modern French politics.

II. Constitutional Status and Role

A. Type of System

France is a unitary republic. The Constitution officially describes it as an "indivisible, secular, democratic and social Republic."[6] The Fifth Republic is often considered to be a "semipresidential" regime.[7] This is in contrast to parliamentary regimes such as the United Kingdom and France's own Third and Fourth Republics, where the government truly revolves around the legislative branch, but also in contrast with presidential regimes such as the United States, which are characterized by a more strict separation of powers.[8] France's semipresidential system features a two-headed executive: a President of the Republic, who is directly elected and holds considerable power, and a Prime Minister, who is appointed by the President but is accountable to the Parliament.[9] Another term often used to describe the French constitutional arrangement is "rationalized parliamentarism."[10] In any case, the drafters of the 1958 Constitution sought to preserve the generally parliamentarian character of France's government, while at the same time limiting the Parliament's power enough to avoid the chronic governmental instability of the Third and Fourth Republics.[11]

---

[3] Id.

[4] Id.

[5] Id.; CONSTITUTION, http://www.legifrance.gouv.fr/affichTexte.do?cidTexte=LEGITEXT000006071194, archived at https://perma.cc/2FRL-GSPB, English translation available at http://www.conseil-constitutionnel.fr/conseil-constitutionnel/english/constitution/constitution-of-4-october-1958.25742.html, archived at https://perma.cc/F6F9-NL79.

[6] CONST. art. 1.

[7] DAVID MARRANI, DYNAMICS IN THE FRENCH CONSTITUTION 13 (2013).

[8] Id.

[9] Id. at 14; CONST. arts. 5–23.

[10] Comment caractériser le régime politique de la Ve République? [How Can the Political Regime of the Vth Republic be Defined?], VIE-PUBLIQUE.FR (official web portal of the French administration) (Jan. 2, 2014), http://www.vie-publique.fr/decouverte-institutions/institutions/veme-republique/transformations/comment-caracteriser-regime-politique-ve-republique.html, archived at https://perma.cc/JN43-2QSV.

[11] Id.

B. Parliament's Place in the French Governance Structure: The Relationship and Overlap Between the Executive and Legislative Branches

The relationship between the legislature and the executive is perhaps more complex in France than in purely parliamentarian systems or presidential systems. The French Parliament does not enjoy the primacy that the British Parliament enjoys in the United Kingdom, and must engage with the executive as a separate branch of government. Yet at the same time, the branches of government are not as strictly separated in France as they are in the United States, for example. Both the French and the American systems of government rely on checks and balances, but whereas the American system is defined by separation of powers, the French constitutional arrangement rests on a structure of interconnecting powers. The main features of this structure of interconnecting powers are the following:

1. Impeachment

The office of President is largely shielded from both parliamentary and judicial interference. Indeed, the President may not be prosecuted while in office except by the International Criminal Court, nor can he be held liable for acts carried out in his official capacity or be compelled to testify before any court or administrative authority.[12] Furthermore, the Parliament may only impeach the President for "breach of his duties patently incompatible with his continuing office,"[13] something which has never occurred so far under the current Constitution.

2. Dissolution

The President may dissolve one of the two chambers of Parliament—the National Assembly (the Senate, however, cannot be dissolved).[14] Elections for a new National Assembly must occur no less than twenty days and no more than forty days following such a dissolution, and the President is barred from dissolving the National Assembly again for a year following these elections.[15] This prerogative was used twice by President Charles de Gaulle (in 1962 and 1968), twice by President François Mitterand (in 1981 and 1988), and once by President Jacques Chirac (in 1997).[16]

3. The Prime Minister and Votes of No Confidence

The office of the Prime Minister, and more broadly the cabinet of which he is the head (usually referred to as "the Government" in France[17]), is the main institution where the President's and the Parliament's powers meet and overlap. The Government is in charge of the day-to-day

---

[12] CONST. arts. 53-2, 67.

[13] *Id.* art. 68.

[14] *Id.* art. 12.

[15] *Id.*

[16] LOUIS FAVOREU ET AL., DROIT CONSTITUTIONNEL [CONSTITUTIONAL LAW] 689 (2011).

[17] *Id.*

administration of government, and of carrying out the nation's policies.[18] Furthermore, most of the President's instruments of power (such as decrees) must be signed by the Prime Minister and by any other minister who might be involved in carrying out the measure in question.[19] Thus, the President cannot do much without the Prime Minister.

The Prime Minister and all cabinet ministers serve at the President's discretion.[20] It is the President who appoints and dismisses them, and he/she can legally choose whomever he/she wishes.[21] However, the Prime Minister needs the support of the Parliament. Not only is that support needed to pass legislation, but the National Assembly also has the power to force the Government's resignation. This is done in one of two ways: either on the Prime Minister's own initiative, or on the National Assembly's initiative.

In the first scenario, the Prime Minister demands a vote of confidence after making a policy statement (either a detailed policy program or a more general statement).[22] Prime Ministers usually call for such votes of confidence as a way to test legislative support for their political program, and/or as a way to solidify support, by "forcing" allied legislators to either go on record as supporting the Government or cause a political crisis. The Prime Minister and his/her Government must resign if they lose the vote, but will generally come out politically strengthened if they win.[23] Many Prime Ministers have demanded votes of confidence throughout the history of the Fifth Republic, and none has lost so far.[24]

In the second scenario, a group representing at least one-tenth of the members of the National Assembly can call for a vote of confidence in the Government.[25] The vote then takes place at least forty-eight hours after the resolution has been tabled, and only votes cast in favor of the no-confidence resolution are counted.[26] In order to prevent the abuse of such no-confidence resolutions, no member of the National Assembly may sign more than three during a single ordinary session, or more than one during a single extraordinary session.[27] This instrument has been widely used by opposition parties to express their disapproval of government policies, but it is in practice more symbolic than effective: out of the many no-confidence resolutions that have been considered since 1958, only one was successful, on October 9, 1962 (the resulting political crisis led then-President Charles de Gaulle to dissolve the National Assembly four days later).[28]

---

[18] CONST. art. 20.

[19] *Id.* art. 19.

[20] *Id.* art. 8.

[21] DAVID MARRANI, DYNAMICS IN THE FRENCH CONSTITUTION 17 (2013).

[22] CONST. art. 49.

[23] FAVOREU ET AL., *supra* note 16, at 768–69.

[24] *Id.*

[25] CONST. art. 49.

[26] *Id.*

[27] *Id.*

[28] FAVOREU ET AL., *supra* note 16, at 770–71.

4. *Shared Legislative Initiative*

The authority to initiate legislation is shared between the Prime Minister (who is appointed by the President, as mentioned above) and the members of the Parliament.[29] The terminology changes a bit according to whether a bill is initiated by the Prime Minister (in which case the term used is *projet de loi* – "law project"), or by a member of the Parliament (the term then used is *proposition de loi* – "law proposal").[30]

5. *The Absence of Presidential Veto Power*

Contrary to the President of the United States, the French President does not have the power to veto legislation. He/she is required to promulgate Acts of Parliament within fifteen days of their final passage.[31] The most he/she can do is ask the Parliament to reopen the debate on the Act or any part thereof.[32]

C. Constitutional Powers and Areas of Responsibility

The Constitution states that the role of Parliament is to "pass statutes," "monitor the action of the Government," and "assess public policies."[33] The Parliament does not have the authority to legislate on anything it wishes, however. Indeed, the Constitution explicitly defines what can be the object of a statute. The areas that fall under the Parliament's legislative authority include the following:

- civic rights and the fundamental guarantees granted to citizens for the exercise of their civil liberties; freedom, pluralism and the independence of the media; the obligations imposed for the purposes of national defense upon the person and property of citizens;

- nationality, the status and capacity of persons, matrimonial property systems, inheritance and gifts;

- the determination of serious crimes and other major offences and the penalties they carry; criminal procedure; amnesty; the setting up of new categories of courts and the status of members of the Judiciary;

- the base, rates and methods of collection of all types of taxes; the issuing of currency.

. . .

- the system for electing members of the Houses of Parliament, local assemblies and the representative bodies for French nationals living abroad, as well as the conditions for holding elective offices and positions for the members of the deliberative assemblies of the territorial communities;

---

[29] CONST. art. 39.

[30] FAVOREU ET AL., *supra* note 16, at 836.

[31] CONST. art. 10.

[32] *Id.*

[33] *Id.* art. 24.

- the setting up of categories of public legal entities;

- the fundamental guarantees granted to civil servants and members of the Armed Forces;

- nationalisation of companies and the transfer of ownership of companies from the public to the private sector.

Statutes shall also lay down the basic principles of :

- the general organisation of national defence;

- the self-government of territorial communities, their powers and revenue;

- education;

- the preservation of the environment;

- systems of ownership, property rights and civil and commercial obligations;

- Employment law, Trade Union law and Social Security;

[- Appropriations][34]

In addition, the French Parliament is responsible for authorizing declarations of war,[35] and for authorizing the extension of a state of siege beyond twelve days (the Council of Ministers, presided over by the President, has the authority to decree a state of siege for those first twelve days).[36] The Constitution specifies that this list may be completed by an "institutional Act" (*Loi organique*).[37] However, any subject that is not enumerated as a legislative matter by the Constitution or an "institutional Act" is considered to be a matter for regulation by the executive, but not for legislation by the Parliament.[38]

The Parliament may also adopt resolutions on any topic, so long as the resolution cannot be considered as an injunction to the Government or a motion of no confidence in the Government.[39] These resolutions are seen as a means of expression for the Parliament and are not binding.[40]

---

[34] *Id.* art. 34.

[35] *Id.* art. 35.

[36] *Id.* art. 36.

[37] *Id.* art. 34.

[38] *Id.* art. 37.

[39] *Id.* art. 34-1.

[40] FAVOREU ET AL., *supra* note 16, at 762.

III. Structure and Composition

A. Structure

1. Overall Structure

France has a bicameral Parliament, composed of the National Assembly and the Senate.[41] The two houses both sit in Paris, but in separate places: the National Assembly at the Bourbon Palace (Palais Bourbon), and the Senate at the Luxembourg Palace (Palais du Luxembourg).[42]

The National Assembly has 577 members, called deputies (*députés*), and the Senate has 348 senators.[43]

2. The National Assembly

a. The President of the National Assembly

At the beginning of each legislative term, the National Assembly elects a President of the National Assembly.[44] The President of the National Assembly has important powers, and is ranked as the fourth most important figure in the French government hierarchy under the rules of protocol (the first three being the President of the Republic, the Prime Minister, and the President of the Senate).[45]

In addition to presiding over the National Assembly's sessions, the President of the National Assembly has a crucial role in organizing the National Assembly's workload and agenda.[46] Furthermore, he/she appoints three of the nine nonpermanent judges on the Conseil

---

[41] *Fiche de synthèse n°4: L'Assemblée nationale et le Sénat – Caractères généraux du Parlement* [*Factsheet No. 4: The National Assembly and the Senate – General Characteristics of the Parliament*], ASSEMBLEE-NATIONALE.FR (website of the National Assembly) (Apr. 15, 2014), http://www2.assemblee-nationale.fr/decouvrir-l-assemblee/role-et-pouvoirs-de-l-assemblee-nationale/les-institutions-francaises-generalites/l-assemblee-nationale-et-le-senat-caracteres-generaux-du-parlement, *archived at* https://perma.cc/WB6C-J7GX.

[42] *Id.*

[43] CONST. art. 24; *Fiche de synthèse n°1: Présentation synthétique des institutions françaises* [*Factsheet No. 1: Summary Presentation of the French Institutions*], ASSEMBLEE-NATIONALE.FR (Apr. 15, 2014), http://www2.assemblee-nationale.fr/decouvrir-l-assemblee/role-et-pouvoirs-de-l-assemblee-nationale/les-institutions-francaises-generalites/presentation-synthetique-des-institutions-francaises, *archived at* https://perma.cc/7U94-UR4N.

[44] CONST. art. 33

[45] *Fiche de synthèse n°19: Le Président de l'Assemblée nationale* [*Factsheet No. 19: The President of the National Assembly*], ASSEMBLEE-NATIONALE.FR (Apr. 15, 2014), http://www2.assemblee-nationale.fr/decouvrir-l-assemblee/role-et-pouvoirs-de-l-assemblee-nationale/les-organes-de-l-assemblee-nationale/le-president-de-l-assemblee-nationale, *archived at* https://perma.cc/CV6X-TR9W; Décret n°89-655 du 13 septembre 1989 relatif aux cérémonies publiques, préséances, honneurs civils et militaires [Decree No. 89-655 of September 13, 1989, Regarding Public Ceremonies, Precedence, Military and Civilian Honors] art. 2, http://www.legifrance.gouv.fr/affichTexte.do?cidTexte=JORFTEXT000000332354&dateText, *archived at* https://perma.cc/JCC3-MYKN.

[46] *Fiche de synthèse n°19: Le Président de l'Assemblée nationale, supra* note 45.

constitutionnel (Constitutional Council, which verifies the constitutionality of French laws), as well as one or several members of various independent agencies such as the Conseil supérieur de l'audiovisuel (Superior Council on Audiovisual Media, France's main regulatory agency for electronic media), the governing council of the Banque de France (the French central bank), the Autorité des marchés financiers (Financial Markets Authority), and several others.[47] He/she also has the authority to ask the Conseil constitutionnel to evaluate the constitutionality of a bill before it becomes law (the only others who may do that are the President of the Republic, the Prime Minister, the President of the Senate, or a group of sixty deputies or sixty senators).[48]

b. The Bureau of the National Assembly

The President of the National Assembly is the head of the Bureau of the National Assembly, and the only member of that body to be elected for an entire legislative term.[49] The other members (six vice-presidents, three quaestors, and twelve secretaries) are elected at the beginning of each year. The National Assembly Rules call for the deputies to choose a bureau that is gender-balanced and that reflects the political composition of the National Assembly as a whole, thus ensuring that opposition parties are adequately represented.[50]

The Bureau is responsible for organizing the National Assembly's workload and agenda, and for managing the institution's day-to-day operations.[51]

c. Permanent Commissions

The National Assembly has eight permanent commissions: the Education and Cultural Commission; the Economic Commission; the Foreign Relations Commission; the Social Issues Commission; the National Defense and Armed Forces Commission; the Sustainable Development and Territorial Organization Commission; the Finance, General Economy, and Budgetary Control Commission; and the Commission for Constitutional Laws, Legislation, and the General Administration of the Republic.[52] Additionally, the National Assembly can also

---

[47] *Id.*; CONST. art. 56.

[48] CONST. art. 61.

[49] *Fiche de synthèse n°20: Le Bureau de l'Assemblée nationale* [*Factsheet No. 20: The Bureau of the National Assembly*], ASSEMBLEE-NATIONALE.FR (Apr. 15, 2014), http://www2.assemblee-nationale.fr/decouvrir-l-assemblee/role-et-pouvoirs-de-l-assemblee-nationale/les-organes-de-l-assemblee-nationale/le-bureau-de-l-assemblee-nationale, *archived at* https://perma.cc/HYN3-7APG.

[50] Règlement de l'Assemblée nationale [Rules of the National Assembly] art. 10 (Jan. 2015), http://www.assemblee-nationale.fr/connaissance/reglement_2015_01.pdf, *archived at* https://perma.cc/Z5D2-PH7T.

[51] *Id.* art. 14; *Fiche de synthèse n°20: Le Bureau de l'Assemblée nationale*, *supra* note 49.

[52] CONST. art. 43; *Fiche de synthèse n°24: Les commissions permanentes* [*Factsheet No. 24: The Permanent Commissions*], ASSEMBLEE-NATIONALE.FR (Apr. 15, 2014), http://www2.assemblee-nationale.fr/decouvrir-l-assemblee/role-et-pouvoirs-de-l-assemblee-nationale/les-organes-de-l-assemblee-nationale/les-commissions-permanentes, *archived at* https://perma.cc/3ZG3-TL42.

create temporary special commissions.[53] A deputy may not be a member of more than one commission at a time.[54]

The main role of these commissions is to prepare bills for full deliberation.[55] Indeed, the Constitution requires that bills be discussed by a commission before being debated and voted on by the full National Assembly.[56] Commissions have the power to amend a bill.[57] Furthermore, in addition to this crucial legislative role, the permanent commissions are supposed to monitor the actions of the government, and to act as the National Assembly's principal fact-finding bodies.[58]

d. Political Groups

Deputies may organize into political groups, although such groups must have at least fifteen members to be officially recognized.[59] These groups represent "the organized expression of the political parties and formations within the Assembly, and allow deputies to group themselves according to their affinities."[60] A deputy may only belong to one political group at a time.[61]

Currently, out of the 577 members of the National Assembly, 287 are affiliated with the Socialiste, républicain et citoyen (Socialist, Republican and Citizen, related to the Socialist Party) political group, 199 are affiliated with Les Républicains (The Republicans, named after the main center-right party that most of its members hail from), and twenty-nine are affiliated with the Union des démocrates et indépendants (Union of Democrats and Independents, related to the centrist political party of the same name) group. Fifty-one deputies are affiliated with one of three smaller political groups, and eleven deputies are unaffiliated.[62]

---

[53] *Id.*

[54] *Id.*

[55] *Id.*

[56] CONST. arts. 42, 43.

[57] *Id.* art. 44.

[58] *Fiche de synthèse n°24: Les commissions permanentes, supra* note 52.

[59] Règlement de l'Assemblée nationale, *supra* note 50, art. 19.

[60] *Fiche de synthèse n°22: Les groupes politiques [Factsheet No. 22: The Political Groups]*, ASSEMBLEE-NATIONALE.FR (Apr. 16, 2014), http://www2.assemblee-nationale.fr/decouvrir-l-assemblee/role-et-pouvoirs-de-l-assemblee-nationale/les-organes-de-l-assemblee-nationale/les-groupes-politiques, *archived at* https://perma.cc/V63W-ZABH.

[61] *Id.*

[62] *Groupes Politiques [Political Groups]*, ASSEMBLEE-NATIONALE.FR, http://www.assemblee-nationale fr/14/tribun/xml/effectifs_groupes.asp (last visited Dec. 18, 2015), *archived at* https://perma.cc/ED3C-XT9A.

3. The Senate

The Senate is organized in a manner very similar to the National Assembly.

a. The President of the Senate

The President of the Senate is elected every three years, after each partial renewal of the Senate (see Part IV, "Elections," below).[63] He/she is in charge of ensuring the Senate's security and proper operation, and has a key role in organizing the institution's workload and agenda.[64] He/she appoints three of the nine nonpermanent judges on the Conseil constitutionnel and, as noted above, he/she is one of the few individuals with the authority to ask the Conseil constitutionnel to evaluate the constitutionality of a bill before it becomes law.[65]

Although he/she is third under the rules of protocol, the President of the Senate is actually next in the line of succession as Head of State in case of absence or incapacity of the President of the Republic.[66] If the President of the Republic is declared permanently absent or incapacitated by the Conseil constitutionnel, the President of the Senate takes on his/her role until new elections are held (at least twenty days, and no more than thirty-five days, after the declaration of vacancy or incapacity).[67] The only presidential prerogatives that the President of the Senate cannot exercise as interim Head of State are the ability to dissolve the National Assembly and the ability to call for a national referendum.[68]

b. The Bureau of the Senate, Commissions, and Political Groups

The Bureau of the Senate is composed of twenty-six members: the President of the Senate, eight vice-presidents, three quaestors, and fourteen secretaries.[69] A new Bureau is formed every three years, with the election of a new President of the Senate.[70] Senate Rules require that the Bureau reflect the political composition of the Senate.[71] Like its equivalent in the National Assembly, the Bureau of the Senate is responsible for organizing the institution's workload and agenda, and for managing day-to-day operations.[72]

---

[63] *Organisation du Sénat [Organization of the Senate]*, SENAT.FR (website of the Senate), http://www.senat.fr/role/orga.html#c580673 (last visited Dec. 17, 2015), *archived at* https://perma.cc/LZR6-SR4T.

[64] *Id.*

[65] CONST. arts. 56, 61.

[66] *Id.* art. 7.

[67] *Id.*

[68] *Id.*

[69] *Le Bureau du Sénat [The Bureau of the Senate]*, SENAT.FR, http://www.senat.fr/role/fiche/bur.html (last visited Dec. 17, 2015), *archived at* https://perma.cc/4PXC-FNRX.

[70] *Id.*

[71] *Id.*

[72] *Id.*

The Senate has seven permanent commissions: the Economic Commission; the Foreign Relations, Defense, and Armed Forces Commission; the Social Issues Commission; the Culture, Education, and Communications Commission; the Territorial Organization and Sustainable Development Commission; the Finance Commission; and the Commission on Constitutional Laws, Legislation, Universal Suffrage, Rules, and General Administration.[73] The Senate also has a Commission on European Affairs to monitor the activities of European Union institutions, and can create special commissions and fact-finding commissions for specific issues.[74] The Senate's commissions have the same powers and responsibilities as their National Assembly equivalents.[75]

Senators can organize into political groups in the same manner as their National Assembly colleagues, except that the threshold number to be officially recognized as a group in the Senate is ten.[76] Currently, 144 senators are affiliated with the Groupe Les Républicains, 110 are affiliated with the Groupe socialiste et républicain, forty-two are affiliated with the Groupe Union des Démocrates et Independants, forty-six senators are affiliated with one of three smaller political groups, and six senators are unaffiliated.[77]

IV. Elections

Deputies are elected by direct universal suffrage for terms of five years (unless the President ends a term prematurely by calling for early elections).[78] Senators, by contrast, are elected by indirect suffrage: they are considered the representatives of the local and regional communities (*communautés territoriales*) of France, and as such are elected by an electoral college of approximately 160,000 "great electors" (*grands electeurs*), 95% of whom are members of the municipal councils of France's 36,767 cities, towns, and villages.[79] Senators are elected for terms of six years, with elections for alternating halves of the Senate being held every three years.[80]

---

[73] *Id.*

[74] *Id.*

[75] *Les commissions permanentes [The Permanent Commissions]*, SENAT.FR, http://www.senat.fr/role/fiche/comperm.html (last visited Dec. 17, 2015), *archived at* https://perma.cc/8UC5-BJ5P.

[76] *Organisation du Sénat, supra* note 63.

[77] *Groupes politiques [Political Groups]*, SENAT.FR (Dec. 14, 2015), http://www.senat.fr/grp, *archived at* https://perma.cc/JLW7-UFF5.

[78] *Fiche de synthèse n°1: Présentation synthétique des institutions françaises, supra* note 43.

[79] *Id.*; *Qu'est-ce qu'une commune? [What is a Municipality?]*, VIE-PUBLIQUE.FR (Web portal of the French Administration) (Jan. 20, 2015), http://www.vie-publique.fr/decouverte-institutions/institutions/collectivites-territoriales/categories-collectivites-territoriales/qu-est-ce-qu-commune.html, *archived at* https://perma.cc/BH4B-PWPW; SÉNAT – L'ESSENTIEL [SENATE – THE BASICS] 8 (July 2015), http://www.senat.fr/fileadmin/Fichiers/Images/visite/Essentiel/Brochure2015-Essentiel-Octobre2015.pdf, *archived at* https://perma.cc/5B45-KWEX.

[80] *Fiche de synthèse n°1: Présentation synthétique des institutions françaises, supra* note 43.

Deputies are elected to discrete, single-seat legislative districts.[81] The number of legislative districts in each *département* (the main administrative subdivision of French territory) varies according to census population. Thus, the number of deputies per département varies from one (in the more rural départements such as Creuse or Lozère) to twenty-one (in the Nord, France's most populous département).[82] Deputies are elected through a two-round voting system.[83]

Senators are distributed by département, with the number of senators per département varying from one for each of the more rural départements, to eleven for Nord and twelve for Paris.[84] Départements that have only one or two senators elect them via a two-round voting system, but those that have three or more senators elect them through a proportional representation system.[85]

Legislative districts are defined by law, as is the number of senators per département.[86] However, the Conseil constitutionnel has ruled that, under the principle of equality of suffrage, these questions must be defined according to neutral, "essentially demographic" criteria.[87] This constitutional rule therefore makes it impossible for any dominant party to engage in gerrymandering.

Contrary to the United States, French citizens residing abroad are represented in Parliament, by eleven deputies and twelve senators.[88]

Although deputies and senators are elected by discrete legislative districts or départements, they are not considered to be the representatives of their specific districts or départements. Rather,

---

[81] *Fiche de synthèse n°14: L'élection des députés* [*Factsheet No. 14: The Election of Deputies*], ASSEMBLEE-NATIONALE.FR (Apr. 15, 2014), http://www2.assemblee-nationale.fr/decouvrir-l-assemblee/role-et-pouvoirs-de-l-assemblee-nationale/le-depute/l-election-des-deputes, *archived at* https://perma.cc/2KDZ-T8KT; SENAT – L'ESSENTIEL, *supra* note 79.

[82] *Fiche de synthèse n°14: L'élection des députés, supra* note 81; Ordonnance n° 2009-935 du 29 juillet 2009 portant répartition des sièges et délimitation des circonscriptions pour l'élection des députés [Ordinance No. 2009-935 of July 29, 2009, Establishing the Distribution of Seats and Boundaries of Voting Districts for the Elections of Deputies], Table No. 2, http://www.legifrance.gouv.fr/affichTexte.do?cidTexte=JORFTEXT000020915491&categorieLien=id, *archived at* https://perma.cc/M46V-E2TS.

[83] *Fiche de synthèse n°14: L'élection des députés, supra* note 81.

[84] SÉNAT – L'ESSENTIEL, *supra* note 79, at 8–9.

[85] *Id.* at 8.

[86] CONST. art. 25; *Fiche de synthèse n°14: L'élection des députés, supra* note 81.

[87] Conseil constitutionnel, Decision No. 86-208 DC, July 2, 1986, http://www.conseil-constitutionnel.fr/conseil-constitutionnel/francais/les-decisions/acces-par-date/decisions-depuis-1959/1986/86-208-dc/decision-n-86-208-dc-du-2-juillet-1986.8273.html, *archived at* https://perma.cc/9J7C-9A37; Conseil constitutionnel, Decision No. 86-218 DC, Nov. 18, 1986, http://www.conseil-constitutionnel.fr/conseil-constitutionnel/francais/les-decisions/acces-par-date/decisions-depuis-1959/1986/86-218-dc/decision-n-86-218-dc-du-18-novembre-1986.8291.html, *archived at* https://perma.cc/YM8C-A8JT; FAVOREU ET AL., *supra* note 16, at 606.

[88] CONST. art. 24; *La représentation des Français établis hors de France* [*Representation of French Citizens Residing Abroad*], SENAT.FR (Dec. 16, 2015), http://www.senat.fr/role/fiche/franc_etrang.html, *archived at* https://perma.cc/XXB9-VYRG.

the constitutional mandate of every deputy and senator is to be a representative of the French Nation as a whole.[89]

V. Legislative Process

The French legislative process has three basic phases: submission, discussion, and promulgation.[90]

A. Submission

A bill may be submitted by the Prime Minister, by a deputy or group of deputies, or by a senator or group of senators.[91] However, only the Prime Minister may submit a bill or an amendment which, if it were to be adopted, would cause either a reduction in public resources or an increase in spending.[92] In practice, the majority of bills are submitted by the Prime Minister.[93]

The Prime Minister, the President of the National Assembly, or the President of the Senate may block the submission of a bill that does not fall within the enumerated matters that, under the Constitution, may be the subject of legislation.[94] The Conseil constitutionnel is the arbiter of any disagreement between the Prime Minister and either chamber of Parliament on whether a bill falls within the proper ambit for legislation.[95]

Appropriations bills, and bills on the financing of social security, must be submitted to the National Assembly first, while bills regarding the territorial organization of France must be submitted to the Senate first.[96]

B. Discussion

Upon submission to either the National Assembly or the Senate, a bill is published and sent to either a permanent commission or a special commission, which studies it and prepares a report.[97] The commission may reject the bill, adopt it as is, or amend it—except for constitutional reforms, appropriations bills, and bills on the financing of social security, which may not be

---

[89] CONST. art. 27; FAVOREU ET AL., *supra* note 16, at 744.

[90] *Fiche de synthèse n°32 : La procédure législative* [*Factsheet No. 32: The Legislative Procedure*], ASSEMBLEE-NATIONALE.FR (Apr. 28, 2014), http://www2.assemblee-nationale.fr/decouvrir-l-assemblee/role-et-pouvoirs-de-l-assemblee-nationale/les-fonctions-de-l-assemblee-nationale/les-fonctions-legislatives/la-procedure-legislative, *archived at* https://perma.cc/CMX2-KQ4Z.

[91] *Id.*; CONST. art. 38.

[92] CONST. art. 40.

[93] *La procédure legislative* [*The Legislative Procedure*], SENAT.FR, http://www.senat.fr/role/fiche/procedure_leg.html (last visited Dec. 18, 2015), *archived at* https://perma.cc/49G2-ETRF.

[94] CONST. art. 41.

[95] *Id.*

[96] *Id.* art. 39.

[97] *Fiche de synthèse n°32: La procédure législative, supra* note 90.

amended in commission.[98] If the bill is approved by the commission (either in its original draft or as amended), or if the commission fails to act on the bill, it is then discussed in a plenary session, where it may again be rejected, adopted as-is, or amended.[99] If the bill is adopted in plenary session, it is then sent to the other chamber of Parliament, where it follows the same basic procedure (discussion and vote in commission, and then in plenary session).[100]

A bill must be adopted in identical terms by both chambers of Parliament to become law.[101] If the two chambers of Parliament fail to adopt an identical bill after two rounds (or one round if the Prime Minister opted for an accelerated procedure and the Presidents of the National Assembly and of the Senate do not jointly deny the Prime Minister's motion), the bill may be sent to a joint commission made up of seven deputies and seven senators. [102] The joint commission is supposed to negotiate and elaborate a common draft for the parts of the bill that the two chambers disagree on. If a compromise is found, it is sent to both the National Assembly and the Senate for final votes, and no further amendment is possible without the Prime Minister's approval.[103] If the joint commission's compromise draft is again rejected by one of the two chambers of Parliament, the Prime Minister may, after a new reading and vote in each chamber, ask for the National Assembly to take a final vote either on the joint commission's final text, or on the last draft that the National Assembly voted on, as amended by the Senate.[104] If the joint commission fails to come to a compromise, the Prime Minister may, after a new reading and vote in each chamber, ask for the National Assembly to take a final vote on the last draft that the National Assembly voted on, as amended by the Senate.[105]

Since 1959, approximately 20% of bills have had to go to a joint commission, and the joint committees have been able to find compromises approximately 60% of the time.[106] Thus, while the National Assembly ends up having the last word in cases of extreme deadlock, such situations have historically been rare.

C. Promulgation

When a bill has been adopted by both chambers of Parliament, the President of the Republic has fifteen days to either promulgate it, or to ask the Parliament to reexamine it.[107] This second option has been very rarely used since 1958.[108] Furthermore, the President of the Republic, the

---

[98] *Id.*; CONST. arts. 42, 43.

[99] CONST. art. 42.

[100] *Fiche de synthèse n°32 : La procédure législative, supra* note 90; *La procédure législative, supra* note 93.

[101] CONST. art. 45.

[102] *Id.*; *La procédure législative, supra* note 93.

[103] *La procédure législative, supra* note 93; FAVOREU ET AL., *supra* note 16, at 851.

[104] *La procédure législative, supra* note 93; FAVOREU ET AL., *supra* note 16, at 852.

[105] *La procédure législative, supra* note 93; FAVOREU ET AL., *supra* note 16, at 852.

[106] FAVOREU ET AL., *supra* note 16, at 851.

[107] CONST. art. 10

[108] *La procédure législative, supra* note 93.

Prime Minister, the President of either chamber of Parliament, or a group of sixty deputies or sixty senators, may ask the Conseil constitutionnel to review a bill's constitutionality before promulgation.[109] The Conseil constitutionnel normally has one month to review the bill, during which time the fifteen-day timeframe to promulgate the bill is temporarily suspended.[110]

The President of the Republic promulgates a new law by signing a promulgation decree, which certifies that the law has been adopted according to the proper constitutional procedure, and which authorizes its publication in the official gazette.[111] The new law then usually comes into force either on the date specified in the law if it contains an effective date provision, or on the day following its publication in the official gazette if the law is silent on that question.[112]

---

[109] CONST. art. 61.

[110] *Id.*

[111] FAVOREU ET AL., *supra* note 16, at 855.

[112] CODE CIVIL [CIVIL CODE] art. 1, http://www.legifrance.gouv.fr/affichCodeArticle.do;jsessionid=EB8F1D B670794AE5C00FD872E7A105D3.tpdila18v_2?cidTexte=LEGITEXT000006070721&idArticle=LEGIARTI0000 06419280&dateTexte=20151218&categorieLien=id#LEGIARTI000006419280, *archived at* https://perma.cc/E85S-WVD6.

Germany

Jenny Gesley
Foreign Law Specialist

SUMMARY   Germany is a federal republic with sixteen states and a parliamentary system. The German Bundestag (Parliament), the main legislative organ, had its inaugural meeting in 1949. The first all-German session of Parliament took place after German reunification in December 1990. The German Bundesrat is the constitutional body through which the states participate in the legislative process. Elections for the Bundestag take place every four years. Seats are allocated according to a personalized proportional voting system that combines a personal vote for a particular candidate in a district (first vote) with a party vote (second vote).

I. Background

A. General History

After the total and unconditional surrender of Germany at the end of the Second World War, the Allied forces consisting of the governments of the United States, the United Kingdom, the former Soviet Union (USSR), and the Provisional Government of the French Republic assumed "supreme authority with respect to Germany, including all the powers possessed by the German government, the High Command, and any state, municipal, or local government or authority."[1] The exercise of supreme authority was conferred upon the Allied Control Council.[2] In the London Protocol of 1944, the governments of the US, UK, and USSR decided that Germany, within the borders as they existed on December 31, 1937, would be divided into three occupation zones, each of which was assigned to one of the three Allied forces. Berlin received a special status under joint occupation of the three forces.[3] On April 8, 1949, the western zones were merged.[4]

---

[1] Declaration Regarding the Defeat of Germany and the Assumption of Supreme Authority with Respect to Germany by the Governments of the United States of America, the Union of Soviet Socialist Republics and the United Kingdom, and the Provisional Government of the French Republic (Berlin Declaration), June 5, 1945, art. 1, 60 Stat. 1649, 68 U.N.T.S. 189, T.I.A.S. 1520, http://www.loc.gov/law/help/us-treaties/bevans/m-ust000003-1140. pdf, *archived at* http://perma.cc/Z7F7-TK9M.

[2] Proclamation No. 1 Establishing the Control Council, Aug. 30, 1945, OFFICIAL GAZETTE OF THE CONTROL COUNCIL FOR GERMANY No. 1, Oct. 29, 1945, pp. 4–5, *available at* http://www.cvce.eu/en/obj/proclamation_no_1_ from_the_control_council_for_germany_berlin_30_august_1945-en-3eac8464-14c7-4e9b-8759-ed51a7ab81ff.html, *archived at* http://perma.cc/7CL2-96Z5.

[3] Protocol Between the Governments of the United States of America, the United Kingdom, and the Union of Soviet Socialist Republics, on the Zones of Occupation in Germany and the Administration of "Greater Berlin" (London Protocol), Sept. 12, 1944, 5 U.S.T. 2078, 227 U.N.T.S. 279, *available at* http://germanhistorydocs.ghi-dc.org/pdf/ eng/Allied%20Policies%201_ENG.pdf, *archived at* http://perma.cc/RJY2-ZH5N.

[4] Agreement as to Tripartite Controls, Apr. 8, 1949, 63 Stat. 2817, 2821, T.I.A.S. 2066, 140 U.N.T.S. 208, http:// www.loc.gov/law/help/us-treaties/bevans/m-ust000004-0832.pdf, *archived at* http://perma.cc/35HV-STC6.

On July 25, 1948, the eleven prime ministers of the German states in the western zones of occupation created a "Council of Experts on Constitutional Matters." The Council met in Herrenchiemsee, Bavaria, from August 10 to August 23, 1948, and was charged by the Allied forces with drawing up a draft constitution for West Germany. In September, the draft was forwarded to the newly convened Parliamentarian Council in Bonn for further consideration by the Council's sixty-five representatives of the German states. On May 8, 1949, the Parliamentarian Council adopted the Basic Law (Grundgesetz) by a vote of 53–12.[5] The Basic Law, which entered into force on May 23, 1949,[6] was proclaimed for all of Germany, East and West, and article 23 of the Basic Law explicitly codified German reunification as a goal.[7]

The Basic Law lays down fundamental rights, establishes the structure and administration of the Federal Republic of Germany, and sets out the legal framework of the three branches of government. The German Bundestag (Parliament) represents the main body of the legislative branch.[8] Elections for the first Bundestag were held on August 14, 1949, and its inaugural meeting took place on September 7, 1949.[9] Following the election of the German President on September 12, 1949, and the election of the German Chancellor on September 15, 1949, the Federal Ministers were appointed on September 20, 1949, thereby completing the establishment of the Federal Republic of Germany.[10]

Even after the Basic Law entered into force, the Allied forces retained occupation powers, which were codified in the Occupation Statute of Germany.[11] The Occupation Statute made every amendment of the Basic Law and adoption of new laws dependent on approval by the Occupation Forces.[12] In an explanatory note accompanying the approval of the Basic Law, the Allied forces also pointed out that Berlin could not be accorded voting membership in the

---

[5] DOKUMENTE DES GETEILTEN DEUTSCHLAND. QUELLENTEXTE ZUR RECHTSLAGE DES DEUTSCHEN REICHES, DER BUNDESREPUBLIK DEUTSCHLAND UND DER DEUTSCHEN DEMOKRATISCHEN REPUBLIK XXV (Ingo von Münch ed., 1968).

[6] GRUNDGESETZ FÜR DIE BUNDESREPUBLIK DEUTSCHLAND [GRUNDGESETZ] [GG] [BASIC LAW], May 23, 1949, BUNDESGESETZBLATT [BGBL] [FEDERAL LAW GAZETTE] I at 1, arts. 38–49, unofficial English translation *at* http://www.gesetze-im-internet.de/englisch_gg/basic_law_for_the_federal_republic_of_germany.pdf, *archived at* http://perma.cc/DEF5-A57P.

[7] Former article 23 of the Basic Law read until 1990 as follows: "This Basic Law applies for the time being only in the states of Baden, Bavaria, Bremen, Greater Berlin, Hamburg, Hesse, Lower Saxony, North Rhine-Westphalia, Rhineland-Palatinate, Schleswig-Holstein, Württemberg-Baden and Württemberg-Hohenzollern. It will enter into force in the other parts of Germany after their accession."

[8] BASIC LAW arts. 38–49.

[9] DOKUMENTE DES GETEILTEN DEUTSCHLAND, *supra* note 5.

[10] *Id.*

[11] Occupation Statute of Germany, May 12, 1949, OFFICIAL GAZETTE OF THE ALLIED HIGH COMMISSION FOR GERMANY, Sept. 23, 1949, No. 1, app., at 13, *available at* http://www.loc.gov/law/help/us-treaties/bevans/m-ust000004-0832.pdf, *archived at* http://perma.cc/35HV-STC6.

[12] *Id.* arts. 4, 5.

Bundestag or Bundesrat or be governed by the Federation of Germany.[13] This situation remained in place until the repeal of the Occupation Statute in 1955.[14]

In 1990, after the fall of the Berlin Wall, the government of the German Democratic Republic (GDR) decided that the GDR would accede to the Federation and adopt the Basic Law according to the procedure set forth in former article 23 of the Basic Law.[15] On August 29, 1990, the Bundestag adopted a law agreeing to the accession.[16] Five weeks after the accession, the first all-German elections took place and the first all-German Bundestag had its inaugural meeting on December 20, 1990.[17]

B. Physical Location of the Parliament

In most countries, the seat of the parliament and the government are located in the capital. Historically, Berlin had been the capital and the seat of the Parliament and the government of the German Empire (1871–1918), of the Weimar Republic (1918–1933), and during National Socialism (1933–1945). The Second World War ended this tradition. Although the Allied Control Council was located in Berlin, it was not possible to locate the seat of the new Bundestag in Berlin owing to Berlin's special legal status as discussed above.

The Parliamentarian Council therefore decided that the seat of the Parliament and the other constitutional organs would be temporarily located in Bonn.[18] On November 3, 1949, the

---

[13] Letter from the Three Western Military Governors to the President of the Parliamentary Council, May 12, 1949, para. 4, *reprinted in* DOKUMENTE DES GETEILTEN DEUTSCHLAND, *supra* note 5, at 130, *available at* http://german historydocs.ghi-dc.org/pdf/eng/Founding%205%20ENG.pdf, *archived at* http://perma.cc/C85P-X33B.

[14] Convention on Relations Between the Three Powers and the Federal Republic of Germany art. 1, para. 2, BGBL. 1954 II at 59 *et seq.*, http://www.bgbl.de/xaver/bgbl/start.xav?startbk=Bundesanzeiger_BGBl&jumpTo=bgbl254s 0057.pdf, *archived at* http://perma.cc/4DUC-NNFL.

[15] Beschluß der Volkskammer der Deutschen Demokratischen Republik über den Beitritt der Deutschen Demokratischen Republik zum Geltungsbereich des Grundgesetzes der Bundesrepublik Deutschland [Decision of the People's Chamber of the German Democratic Republic to Accede to the Jurisdiction of the Basic Law of the Federal Republic of Germany], Aug. 23, 1990, GESETZBLATT DER DEUTSCHEN DEMOKRATISCHEN REPUBLIK [GBL. DDR] [OFFICIAL GAZETTE OF THE GERMAN DEMOCRATIC REPUBLIC] I, No. 57, 4 Sept. 1990, at 1323–24, https:// www.bundesarchiv.de/tools/docview.html?file=/imperia/md/images/abteilungen/abtddr/volkskammerwahl/17_da_1 _4042_blatt_050_801x0_0_16.jpg, *archived at* http://perma.cc/XYE5-HKTP. For the text of article 23 of the Basic Law, see note 7.

[16] Gesetz zu dem Vertrag vom 3. August 1990 zur Vorbereitung und Durchführung der ersten gesamtdeutschen Wahl zwischen der Bundesrepublik Deutschland und derDeutschen Demokratischen Republik sowie dem Änderungsvertrag vom 20. August 1990 [Act on the Agreement of August 3, 1990, to Prepare and Execute the First All-German Elections Between the Federal Republic of Germany and the German Democratic Republic and on the Amending Agreement of August 20, 1990], Aug. 29, 1990, BGBL II, at 813, http://www.bgbl.de/xaver/bgbl/start. xav?startbk=Bundesanzeiger_BGBl&jumpTo=bgbl290s0813.pdf, *archived at* http://perma.cc/D8C4-3M6P.

[17] Michael Kilian, *Der Vorgang der Wiedervereinigung* [*The Process of Reunification*], *in* HANDBUCH DES STAATSRECHTS DER BUNDESREPUBLIK DEUTSCHLAND, BAND I. HISTORISCHE GRUNDLAGEN [HANDBOOK OF CONSTITUTIONAL LAW OF THE FEDERAL REPUBLIC OF GERMANY, VOL. I. HISTORICAL BACKGROUND] 597, 643 (Josef Isensee & Paul Kirchhof eds., 2003).

[18] DER PARLAMENTARISCHE RAT, 1948–1949: AKTEN U. PROTOKOLLE, BAND 9. PLENUM 683 (Deutscher Bundestag & Bundesarchiv eds., 1996).

Bundestag approved the decision of the Parliamentarian Council.[19] In the same session it was decided that "the constitutional organs will move their seat to the capital of Germany, Berlin, once general, free, equal, secret, and free elections were held in all of Berlin and in the Soviet occupied territory."[20] Over the years, the Bundestag reiterated several times its commitment to make Berlin the capital of the German state as a whole and move the seat of the Parliament and other official buildings to Berlin.[21]

In 1990, after German reunification, it was agreed to once again make Berlin the capital of a unified Germany.[22] The designation of Berlin as the capital did not automatically entail a decision on the future location of the Parliament or the government. The Unification Treaty only provided that a decision on the location would be made after unification had been achieved.[23]

After a controversial discussion of the pros and cons, it was agreed to move the seat of the Bundestag from Bonn to Berlin to further German reintegration,[24] and in April 1999 that decision was implemented.[25] The status of Berlin as the capital of Germany was codified in article 22, paragraph 1 of the Basic Law as part of the amendment of the Basic Law in 2006. Today, Berlin again serves as the capital of the Federal Republic of Germany, as well as the seat of the German Bundestag, the German Bundesrat, the Federal President, and the German Government.

---

[19] DEUTSCHER BUNDESTAG: DRUCKSACHEN UND PROTOKOLLE [BT-DRS.] 1/14, pp. 341–43, http://dipbt.bundestag. de/doc/btp/01/01014.pdf, *archived at* http://perma.cc/9737-DELB.

[20] BT-DRS. 1/135, http://dipbt.bundestag.de/doc/btd/01/001/0100135.pdf, *archived at* http://perma.cc/X8VS-HE4B; BT-DRS. 1/143, http://dipbt.bundestag.de/doc/btd/01/001/0100143.pdf, *archived at* http://perma.cc/N5VF-7BTQ; BT-DRS. 1/14, pp. 343–47, http://dipbt.bundestag.de/doc/btp/01/01014.pdf, *archived at* http://perma.cc/9737-DELB.

[21] *See, e.g.*, BT-DRS. 1/63 (1950), p. 2309, http://dipbt.bundestag.de/doc/btp/01/01063.pdf, *archived at* http://perma. cc/N8TG-TVGT; BT-DRS. 2/3116 (1953), http://dipbt.bundestag.de/doc/btd/02/031/0203116.pdf, *archived at* http:// perma.cc/U888-62TE; BT-DRS. 2/190 (1957), p. 10812 *et seq.*, http://dipbt.bundestag.de/doc/btp/02/02190. pdf, *archived at* http://perma.cc/EL6U-4TX3; BT-DRS. 9/43 (1981), p. 2480, http://dipbt.bundestag.de/doc/btp/09/ 09043.pdf, *archived at* http://perma.cc/SLQ2-5E46.

[22] Vertrag zwischen der Bundesrepublik Deutschland und der Deutschen Demokratischen Republik über die Herstellung der Einheit Deutschlands (Einigungsvertrag) [Agreement Between the Federal Republic of Germany and the German Democratic Republic on the Accomplishment of the Unification of Germany (Unification Agreement)], Aug. 31, 1990, BGBL. II at 889, art. 2, para. 1, sentence 1, http://www.gesetze-im-internet.de/ bundesrecht/einigvtr/gesamt.pdf, *archived at* http://perma.cc/W5NB-H8TU, unofficial English translation *at* http://germanhistorydocs.ghi-dc.org/pdf/eng/Unification_Treaty.pdf, *archived at* http://perma.cc/CS23-BZAL.

[23] *Id.*

[24] Vollendung der Einheit Deutschlands, June 19, 1991, BT-DRS. 12/815, http://dipbt.bundestag.de/doc/btd/12/ 008/1200815.pdf, *archived at* http://perma.cc/W77Q-2LRW.

[25] Gesetz zur Umsetzung des Beschlusses des Deutschen Bundestages vom 20. Juni 1991 zur Vollendung der Einheit Deutschlands (Berlin/Bonn-Gesetz) [Act to Implement the Decision of the German Bundestag of June 20, 1991, to Complete the Unification of Germany (Berlin/Bonn Act)], Apr. 6, 1994, BGBL. I at 918, as amended, § 2, para. 1, http://www.gesetze-im-internet.de/bundesrecht/berlin_bonng/gesamt.pdf, *archived at* http://perma.cc/WH 5V-VV6P.

C. Reichstag Building

The German Bundestag is housed in the former Reichstag building, which was designed by Paul Wallot and inaugurated in 1894.[26] The Reichstag building was utilized as the seat of the Parliament of the German Reich (German Empire) and of the Weimar Republic.

On February 27, 1933, the Reichstag building was set on fire in an arson attack. Marinus van der Lubbe, a young Dutch council communist, was arrested and convicted for the crime, but responsibility for the crime has never been clearly established and remains an ongoing topic of debate.[27] The Nazi party took advantage of the situation: Adolf Hitler convinced the German President Hindenburg to issue an emergency decree (Reichstag Fire Decree) and suspend civil liberties.[28]

During the time of the Nazi regime from 1933 to 1945, the Reichstag building was not used as the seat of the Parliament. The plenary chamber had been severely damaged by the fire and was not restored. The remaining rooms, which had been spared by the fire, were used for the administration of the Parliament and the library. In 1940, air-raid shelters for women and children were installed in the basement of the Reichstag building. It was also used by the Central Archives for Military Medicine, the General Building Inspector for the Capitol, the German Committee for Standardization, and the Berlin Charité hospital.[29]

When the Soviet Army entered Berlin, they focused their attacks on the Reichstag building and almost completely destroyed it. The graffiti left on the walls by Soviet soldiers is still visible today, and was preserved as a remembrance of the horrors of the Second World War.[30] On October 26, 1955, the Bundestag decided to restore the building because of its symbolic character for a unified Germany.[31]

After German reunification and the decision to move the seat of Parliament back to Berlin, the Reichstag building was chosen as the future seat of the Bundestag. An architectural design competition was launched and Sir Norman Foster's design was selected.[32] He decided to install

---

[26] NINO GALETTI, DER BUNDESTAG ALS BAUHERR IN BERLIN: IDEEN, KONZEPTE, ENTSCHEIDUNGEN ZUR POLITISCHEN ARCHITEKTUR (1991–1998) [THE BUNDESTAG AS A BUILDER IN BERLIN: IDEAS, CONCEPTS, DECISIONS ON A POLITICAL ARCHITECTURE (1991–1998)] at 75 (2008).

[27] BENJAMIN CARTER HETT, BURNING THE REICHSTAG: AN INVESTIGATION INTO THE THIRD REICH'S ENDURING MYSTERY 19–25 (2014).

[28] Michael S. Cullen, Streit um Symbole [Dispute Over Symbols], in "DEM DEUTSCHEN VOLKE." DER BUNDESTAG IM BERLINER REICHTSTAGSGEBÄUDE ["FOR THE GERMAN PEOPLE." THE BUNDESTAG IN THE BERLIN REICHSTAG BUILDING] 192, 199 (Heinrich Wefing ed., 1999).

[29] Gerhard Hahn, Für Bücher, Kinder, Wöchnerinnen [For Books, Children, Women in Childbed], in "DEM DEUTSCHEN VOLKE," supra note 28, at 46, 56.

[30] Bernhard Schulz, Kosmos der Werte [Cosmos of Values], in "DEM DEUTSCHEN VOLKE," supra note 28, at 211, 222.

[31] BT-DRS. 02/108, p. 5888, http://dipbt.bundestag.de/doc/btp/02/02108.pdf, archived at http://perma.cc/YAU2-SSXA.

[32] GALETTI, supra note 26, at 230.

a publicly accessible glass dome that offers a view into the plenary chamber and of the skyline of Berlin, and represents openness and transparency.[33]

II. Constitutional Status and Role

Germany is a federal republic with sixteen states.[34] It has a parliamentary system in which the main legislative role is assigned to the German Bundestag.[35] The Bundestag is the only constitutional organ that is directly elected by the people.[36]

The German Basic Law does not contain a provision that enumerates the powers and tasks of the Bundestag similar to article I, section 8 of the US Constitution. Individual provisions in the Basic Law also provide only a limited picture of the functions of the Bundestag. The powers and tasks of the Bundestag therefore have to be inferred from the context and purpose of the Basic Law, and from constitutional practice.[37]

A. Legislation

All laws must be adopted by the German Bundestag.[38] It is therefore considered the main legislative body. As Germany is a federation, its sixteen states (*Länder*) participate in the legislative process through another constitutional organ, the German Bundesrat (Federal Council).[39] The Federal Government and the Federal President also participate in the legislative process.[40] Legislative initiatives may start with the Federal Government, in the Bundestag, or in the Bundesrat, and are then debated in the Bundestag.[41] The legislative process is described in greater detail below.

B. Oversight

Besides engaging in the legislative process, the German Bundestag monitors and scrutinizes the government and its work. In order to exercise its oversight function of the executive branch, the Bundestag must be informed about the work of the Federal Government and has several instruments and rights at its disposal to achieve that purpose. The Bundestag can either gather

---

[33] Sir Norman Foster, *Ein optimistisches Zeichen für ein modernes Deutschland* [*An Optimistic Sign for a Modern Germany*] *in* "DEM DEUTSCHEN VOLKE," *supra* note 28, at 180, 185–86.

[34] BASIC LAW art. 20, para. 1.

[35] *Id*. arts. 38–49, 77.

[36] *Id*. arts. 20, para. 1; 38, para. 1.

[37] Siegfried Magiera, *III. Der Bundestag, Art. 38, in* GRUNDGESETZ KOMMENTAR [BASIC LAW COMMENTARY] 1219, para. 21 (Michael Sachs ed., 7th ed. 2014).

[38] BASIC LAW art. 77, para. 1.

[39] *Id*. art. 50.

[40] *Id*. arts. 76–78.

[41] *Id*. art.76.

the information itself by forming permanent and special committees,[42] or it can require the Federal Government to provide the necessary information.[43]

C. Election of the Federal Chancellor and the Federal President

The German Bundestag elects the Federal Chancellor in a secret vote without any prior debate.[44] The person who receives the majority of the votes becomes Federal Chancellor.[45] The Federal Chancellor is the head of government,[46] a position that has been held by Angela Merkel since 2005.[47] The Bundestag can also dismiss the Federal Chancellor by means of a vote of no confidence. The members must elect an alternative candidate by majority vote and request the dismissal of the former Federal Chancellor from the Federal President.[48]

Unlike the US Senate, the Bundestag is not involved in the selection process for Federal Ministers. They are appointed by the Federal President on a binding proposal by the Federal Chancellor.[49]

The Bundestag also participates in the election of the Federal President, who is the head of state and represents the Federal Republic of Germany at home and abroad.[50] The position is currently held by Joachim Gauck.[51] The Federal President is chosen by the Federal Convention by majority vote. The Federal Convention is convened only to elect the Federal President and consists of the members of the Bundestag and an equal number of members elected by the governments of the German states.[52]

III. Structure and Composition

As mentioned in Part II, above, the main legislative organ is the German Bundestag.[53] The Bundesrat is the constitutional body through which the representatives of the German state governments participate in the legislative process.[54] The Basic Law does not use the terms

---

[42] *Id.* art. 45a.

[43] *Id.* art. 43.

[44] *Id.* art. 63, para. 1.

[45] *Id.* art. 63, para. 2.

[46] *Id.* arts. 62, 65.

[47] *Angela Merkel. Biography*, THE FEDERAL CHANCELLOR, http://www.bundeskanzlerin.de/Webs/BKin/EN/AngelaMerkel/Biography/biography_node.html, *archived at* http://perma.cc/7Q5G-NE6M.

[48] BASIC LAW art. 67, para. 1.

[49] *Id.* art. 64, para. 1.

[50] *Id.* art. 59.

[51] *Curriculum vitae of Federal President Joachim Gauck*, DER BUNDESPRÄSIDENT, http://www.bundespraesident.de/EN/Federal-President/CurriculumVitae/curriculumvitae-node.html, *archived at* http://perma.cc/GEC9-53R9.

[52] BASIC LAW art. 54, paras.1, 3.

[53] *Id.* art. 77, para. 1.

[54] *Id.* art. 77, paras. 2–4.

"bicameral parliament" or "upper and lower house" with regard to the Bundestag and Bundesrat. They are both described as "constitutional bodies," as are the Federal President, the Federal Government, the Federal Convention, the Joint Committee,[55] and the Federal Constitutional Court.[56] Furthermore, the Federal Constitutional Court does not consider the Bundesrat an upper house of Parliament because, according to the court, it "does not participate on an equal footing with the German Bundestag in the legislative process" and "does not adopt the laws."[57] For all practical purposes, though, the German system can be described as a bicameral system, in particular in all cases in which legislation requires the consent of the Bundesrat.[58]

A. German Bundestag

1. Members

The German Bundestag has at least 598 members.[59] The number of members fluctuates after every election owing to the voting system, which combines a personal with a party vote.[60] Currently, there are 631 total seats due to four "overhang seats" (*Überhangmandate*) and twenty-nine "balance seats" (*Ausgleichsmandate*).[61] One of the members has stepped down and will not be replaced, so the total number of members is now 630.[62]

2. Seat Allocation

The seat allocation in the German Bundestag corresponds to the number of votes cast for the party with the second vote.[63] The first 299 seats are allocated to the candidates who were elected by personal vote (first vote). The remaining seats are filled from the party lists.[64] In the current Eighteenth German Bundestag, the Christian Democratic Union/Christian Social Union (CDU/CSU) parliamentary group has 310 seats, the Social Democratic Party (SPD) has 193

---

[55] *Id.* art. 53a.

[56] *Id.* art. 92–94.

[57] Bundesverfassungsgericht [BVerfG], 37 ENTSCHEIDUNGEN DES BUNDESVERFASSUNGSGERICHTS [BVERFGE] 363, 380 *et seq.*

[58] Thomas Mann, [Art. 77 Verfahren bei Gesetzesbeschlüssen] [Art. 77 Procedure for Adopting Legislation], *in* GRUNDGESETZ KOMMENTAR, *supra* note 37, at 1614, 1616, para. 2.

[59] Bundeswahlgesetz [BWahlG] [Federal Voting Act], July 23, 1993, BGBL. I at 1288, 1594, as amended, §§ 1, 6, para. 5, http://www.gesetze-im-internet.de/bundesrecht/bwahlg/gesamt.pdf, *archived at* http://perma.cc/QW5Z-3SLL.

[60] BWahlG § 4.

[61] For a discussion of the election system and overhang and balance seats, see Part IV, *infra.*

[62] *Katherina Reiche (Potsdam), CDU/CSU*, DEUTSCHER BUNDESTAG https://www.bundestag.de/bundestag/abgeordnete18/biografien/R/reiche_katharina/258916 (last visited Nov. 30, 2015), *archived at* http://perma.cc/BJN8-G3YP.

[63] BWahlG § 6.

[64] *Id.* § 1, para. 2.

seats, the Left Party has 64 seats, and Alliance '90/The Greens have 63 seats. For the first time since 1949, the Free Democratic Party (FDP) is not represented in the Bundestag.[65]

3. Parliamentary Groups

At least 5% of the members of the German Bundestag may form a parliamentary group (*Fraktion*).[66] The members usually belong to the same party or hold the same political views. If that is not the case, the formation of a parliamentary group requires permission from the Bundestag. The formation of a parliamentary group enables the members to work together to achieve shared goals.

4. Committees

For each electoral term, the Bundestag may set up permanent committees, which roughly correspond to the ministries of the government. The committees prepare the deliberations and decisions of the Bundestag.[67] More specialized committees are set up to deal with specific matters and are dissolved as soon as they have completed their work.[68]

5. Key Leadership Roles

The key leadership role in the German Bundestag is held by the President of the Bundestag.[69] Professor Norbert Lammert has served as President of the German Bundestag since October 2005 and was reelected on October 22, 2013.[70]

The President of the Bundestag represents the Bundestag and therefore the legislative branch in Germany externally. One of his/her main responsibilities is to ensure the maintenance of parliamentary order when the Bundestag is in session.[71]

---

[65] *Distribution of Seats in the 18th German Bundestag*, DEUTSCHER BUNDESTAG, http://www.bundestag.de/htdocs_e/bundestag/plenary/distributionofseats (last updated Sept. 21, 2015), *archived at* http://perma.cc/B77R-N3TL.

[66] Geschäftsordnung des Deutschen Bundestages [BTGO] [Rules of Procedure of the German Bundestag], June 25, 1980, BGBL. I at 1237, § 10, http://www.gesetze-im-internet.de/bundesrecht/btgo_1980/gesamt.pdf, *archived at* http://perma.cc/78QT-J3TR.

[67] BTGO § 54, para. 1.

[68] SUSANNE LINN & FRANK SOBOLEWSKI, THE GERMAN BUNDESTAG – FUNCTIONS AND PROCEDURES 25 *et seq.* (2010), https://www.btg-bestellservice.de/pdf/80080000.pdf, *archived at* http://perma.cc/PH2T-ZQ62.

[69] BASIC LAW art. 40.

[70] *Professor Norbert Lammert, President of the Bundestag*, DEUTSCHER BUNDESTAG, http://www.bundestag.de/htdocs_e/bundestag/presidium/lammert_neu/lammert/246232 (last visited Nov. 30, 2016), *archived at* http://perma.cc/V7GX-S826.

[71] BTGO § 7.

B. German Bundesrat

1. Members and Votes

The German Bundesrat has sixty-nine members consisting of representatives of the state governments.[72] Each German state is awarded at least three votes. States with more than two million inhabitants receive four votes, states with more than six million inhabitants five votes, and states with more than seven million inhabitants six votes.[73] The number of votes determines the number of members that the state can send to the Bundesrat.[74] Each state can cast its vote only en bloc.[75]

2. Party Representation

Because the Bundesrat consists of representatives of the state governments, the political parties represented in the Bundesrat correspond to the current leadership in the state in question and change after elections are held in a state. At present, the composition is as follows: the CSU is represented only in Bavaria, whereas the CDU is represented in the government of six states,[76] the SPD in fourteen states,[77] Alliance '90/The Greens in nine states,[78] the Left Party in two states,[79] and the South Schleswig Voters' Association (SSW) as a party for the Danish minority only in Schleswig-Holstein.[80]

3. Key Leadership Roles

Like the President of the Bundestag, the President of the Bundesrat holds the key leadership role.[81] Every November 1, a Prime Minister from one of the German states is appointed as President of the Bundesrat for a one-year period.[82] The office rotates between the German states based on population size, with the cycle starting with the Prime Minister from the most populous

---

[72] BASIC LAW art. 51.

[73] *Id.* art. 51, para. 2.

[74] *Id.* art. 51, para. 3.

[75] *Id.* art. 51, para. 3, sentence 2.

[76] Berlin, Mecklenburg-West Pomerania, Saarland, Saxony, Saxony-Anhalt, and Hesse.

[77] Berlin, Mecklenburg-West Pomerania, Saarland, Saxony, Saxony-Anhalt, Baden-Württemberg, Brandenburg, Bremen, Hamburg, Lower Saxony, North-Rhine Westphalia, Rhineland-Palatinate, Schleswig-Holstein, and Thuringia.

[78] Baden-Württemberg, Bremen, Hamburg, Hesse, Lower Saxony, North-Rhine Westphalia, Rhineland-Palatinate, Schleswig-Holstein, and Thuringia.

[79] Brandenburg and Thuringia.

[80] *Composition of the Bundesrat*, BUNDESRAT, http://www.bundesrat.de/EN/organisation-en/stimmenverteilung-en/stimmenverteilung-en-node html, *archived at* http://perma.cc/P9GF-9LGX.

[81] BASIC LAW art. 52.

[82] Geschäftsordnung des Bundesrates [BRGO] [Rules of Procedure of the Bundesrat], Nov. 6, 1993, BGBL. I at 2007, as amended, § 5, para. 1, http://www.gesetze-im-internet.de/bundesrecht/brgo_1966/gesamt.pdf, *archived at* http://perma.cc/SHT7-32EJ.

state and moving in descending order to the Prime Minister from the least populous state. The current President of the Bundesrat for the period from November 1, 2015, to October 31, 2016, is Stanislaw Tillich, the Prime Minister of Saxony.[83]

The President of the Bundesrat represents the Bundesrat externally.[84] His main responsibility is to convene and chair the Bundesrat's plenary sessions.[85] Furthermore, if the Federal President is unable to perform his duties or if his office falls prematurely vacant, the President of the Bundesrat exercises the Federal President's powers.[86]

IV. Elections

A. German Bundestag

Germany uses a personalized proportional voting system that combines a personal direct vote for a particular candidate in a district (first vote) with a party vote (second vote).[87] There are 299 electoral districts.[88] A party must receive at least 5% of the second votes or three direct mandates to be represented in the German Bundestag.[89]

Elections for the Bundestag are held every four years.[90] The Basic Law imposes no term limits on members of the Bundestag. The last election took place on September 22, 2013,[91] with a voter turnout of 71.5%.[92] The next election will take place in the fall of 2017, but no specific date has yet been set.

The election law was amended in 2013 after the Federal Constitutional Court had declared the former version of the law unconstitutional owing to the negative vote weight effect caused by the overhang seats.[93] Overhang seats are allocated to a party if, on the basis of the first votes, the number of seats for the party exceeds the number of seats allocated to the party following the

---

[83] *Bundesratspräsident Stanislaw Tillich*, BUNDESRAT, http://www.bundesrat.de/DE/bundesrat/praesidium/praesident/praesident-node.html (last visited Nov. 30, 2015), *archived at* http://perma.cc/R2DL-M9G4.

[84] BRGO § 6, para. 1.

[85] BASIC LAW art. 52, para. 2.

[86] *Id.* art. 57.

[87] BWahlG § 4.

[88] *Id.* § 2, para. 2, in conjunction with the Annex.

[89] *Id.* § 6, para. 3.

[90] *Id.* art. 39, para. 1.

[91] *Election to the 18th German Bundestag,* THE FEDERAL RETURNING OFFICER, http://www.bundeswahlleiter.de/en/bundestagswahlen/BTW_BUND_13/ (last visited Nov. 30, 2015), *archived at* http://perma.cc/3QPR-NUSQ.

[92] *Federal Result, Final Result of the Election to the German Bundestag 2013*, THE FEDERAL RETURNING OFFICER, http://www.bundeswahlleiter.de/en/bundestagswahlen/BTW_BUND_13/ergebnisse/bundesergebnisse/index.html, (last visited Nov. 30, 2015), *archived at* http://perma.cc/P8Y5-VNJN.

[93] BVerfG, 131 BVERFGE 316, http://www.bverfg.de/e/fs20120725_2bvf000311.html, *archived at* http://perma.cc/L53U-WNEK.

second votes.[94] Under the old system, receiving more second votes in one state could potentially cost the party seats in the final allocation of seats for the Bundestag.[95]

According to the current law, the seat allocation for every German state is calculated on the basis of the proportion of the German population living there. Next, the seats in each state are allocated according to the party lists proportionate to the second votes each party receives. In a subsequent step, the minimum number of seats for each party at the federal level is determined by adding up the minimum number of seats in the individual states. The minimum number of seats for a party in a state is either the number of direct votes (first votes) or second votes it receives in that state, whichever is greater. In order to ensure that each party receives seats proportionate to its share at the federal level, additional balance seats are awarded.[96]

The Basic Law mandates that the new German Bundestag must convene no later than the thirtieth day after the elections.[97] During that period, coalition negotiations are held in order to form a government if no single party has received an absolute majority of the votes. The current German government consists of a grand coalition of the CDU/CSU and SPD parties.[98]

B. German Bundesrat

There are no direct elections for the Bundesrat. As mentioned, above, the Bundesrat's composition is determined by the composition of the sixteen German state governments and changes every time elections are held in a German state.

V. Legislative Process

A. Legislative Initiative and Readings

A legislative initiative for a bill can be launched by the Federal Government, the Bundestag, or the Bundesrat.[99] Every bill is read in the Bundestag three times before the final vote.[100] After the initial first debate, the bill is referred to a committee, which reports on the bill and gives a recommendation with regard to adoption.[101] During the second reading, amendments may be proposed.[102] The final discussion takes into account the decisions from the second reading.

---

[94] *Id.* at 316, 321.

[95] *Id.* at 316, 346–47.

[96] BWahlG § 6, paras. 2–7.

[97] BASIC LAW art. 39, para. 2.

[98] Deutschlands Zukunft gestalten, Koalitionsvertrag zwischen CDU, CSU und SPD, 18. Legislaturperiode [Shaping Germany's Future, Coalition Agreement Between CDU, CSU and SPD, 18th Legislative Period], http://www.bundesregierung.de/Content/DE/_Anlagen/2013/2013-12-17-koalitionsvertrag.pdf?_blob=publicationFile&v=2, *archived at* http://perma.cc/4CJS-UQ8M.

[99] BASIC LAW art. 76.

[100] BTGO arts. 78–86.

[101] *Id.* art. 80.

[102] *Id.* art. 82.

Amendments are possible only for changes made during the second phase.[103] Once a bill is adopted by the Bundestag, it is referred to the Bundesrat.[104]

The subsequent procedure differs depending on whether the bill requires the consent of the Bundesrat (*Zustimmungsgesetz*) or not (*Einspruchsgesetz*). The Basic Law exhaustively lists the types of bills that require the consent of the Bundesrat.[105] In general these bills fall into one of three categories: (1) bills that amend the Basic Law, (2) bills that affect the finances of the states, or (3) bills that affect the organizational and administrative jurisdiction of the states.[106]

B. Bills Requiring Consent of the German Bundesrat (*Zustimmungsgesetz*)

If the bill requires the consent of the Bundesrat and the Bundesrat consents, the bill is adopted by the Bundestag.[107]

If the Bundesrat disagrees, it can file a motion for discussion of the bill in the Mediation Committee to find a compromise.[108] The Mediation Committee is composed of sixteen members of the Bundesrat and an equal number of members of the Bundestag.[109] The members of the German Bundestag correspond to the size of the parliamentary groups in the Bundestag. The Mediation Committee can only propose amendments, but cannot adopt a bill itself.

If the Mediation Committee proposes no amendments to the bill and the Bundesrat consents, the Bundestag adopts the bill.[110] If the Bundesrat rejects the bill, the legislative initiative is defeated.[111]

If the Mediation Committee proposes an amendment, the amendment must be put to a vote in the Bundestag again before it can be discussed in the Bundesrat.[112] If the Bundestag rejects the

---

[103] *Id.* art. 85.

[104] BASIC LAW art. 77, para. 1, sentence 2.

[105] *Id.* arts. 16a, paras. 2 & 3; 23, paras. 1 & 7; 29, para. 7; 72, para. 3; 73, para. 2; 74, para. 2; 79, para. 2; 84, paras. 1 & 5; 85, para. 1; 87, para. 3; 87b, paras. 1 & 2; 87c; 87d, para. 2; 87e, para. 5; 87f, para. 1; 91a, para. 2; 96, para. 5; 104a, paras. 4–6; 104b, para. 2; 105, para. 3; 106, paras. 3–6; 106a, sentence 2; 107, para. 1; 108, paras. 2, 4, 5; 109, paras. 3–5; 115c, paras. 1 & 3; 115k, para. 3; 115l, para. 1; 120a, para. 1; 134, para. 4; 135, para. 5; 135a; 143a, para. 1.

[106] *Consent and Objection Bills*, BUNDESRAT, http://www.bundesrat.de/EN/funktionen-en/gesetzgebung-en/zust-einspr-en/zust-einspr-en-node.html (last visited Nov. 30, 2015), *archived at* http://perma.cc/QPF7-R34D.

[107] BASIC LAW art. 78.

[108] *Id.* art. 77, para. 2.

[109] *Id.*; Gemeinsame Geschäftsordnung des Bundestages und des Bundesrates für den Ausschuss nach Artikel 77 GG (Vermittlungsausschuß) [Joint Rules of Procedure of the Bundestag and the Bundesrat for the Committee Established According to Article 77 of the Basic Law (Mediation Committee)] § 1, Apr. 19, 1951, BGBL. II at 103, as amended, http://www.gesetze-im-internet.de/bundesrecht/btbrggo/gesamt.pdf, *archived at* http://perma.cc/97LN-64DM.

[110] BASIC LAW art. 78.

[111] *Id.* art. 77, para. 2a.

[112] *Id.* art. 77, para. 2, sentence 5.

amendment, the bill is defeated. If, on the other hand, the Bundestag accepts the amendment, it refers the amended bill to the Bundesrat. The Bundesrat again has the option to consent so that the amended bill is adopted, or to reject the amended bill so that the amended bill is defeated.

C. Bills Not Requiring Consent of the German Bundesrat (*Einspruchsgesetz*)

If a bill does not require the consent of the Bundesrat, the Bundesrat may still object and file a motion for discussion of the bill in the Mediation Committee.[113]

If the Mediation Committee proposes no amendments and the Bundesrat consents, the bill is adopted. If on the other hand, the Mediation Committee proposes no amendments and the Bundesrat rejects the bill, it is forwarded to the Bundestag. The Bundestag can either overrule the objection of the Bundesrat and adopt the bill or not overrule the objection and defeat the bill.[114]

If the Mediation Committee proposes an amendment, the Bundestag must vote on the changes again.[115] If the Bundestag rejects the amendment, the bill is defeated.

If the Bundestag accepts the amendment, it refers the amended bill back to the Bundesrat. If the Bundesrat also agrees to the changes, the amended bill is adopted. In the event that the Bundesrat rejects the amended bill, the Bundestag has the option to overrule the objection and adopt the bill. If there is no majority in the Bundestag to overrule the objection, the bill is defeated.[116]

D. Signature and Entry into Force

Once an act is adopted by the German Bundestag, the Federal Government forwards it to the Federal President for his/her signature and publication in the *Federal Law Gazette*.[117] An act takes effect on the date specified in the act or, if no date is specified, fourteen days after its publication in the *Federal Law Gazette*.[118]

E. Special Procedures

The provision of the Basic Law dealing with budget law[119] contains a special procedure for expenditure-increasing and revenue-decreasing bills. These bills require the consent of the Federal Government.[120] The Federal Government can also demand that the Bundestag postpone

---

[113] *Id.* art. 77, paras. 2 & 3.

[114] *Id.* art. 77, para. 4.

[115] *Id.* art. 77, para. 2, sentence 5.

[116] *Id.* art. 77, para. 4.

[117] *Id.* art. 82, para. 1.

[118] *Id.* art. 82, para. 2.

[119] *Id.* art. 113.

[120] *Id.* art. 113, para. 1.

its vote on such a bill[121] and demand a second vote on the bill within four weeks after its adoption by the Bundestag.[122]

During a "state of defense,"[123] the Basic Law mandates a simplified legislative procedure.[124] Bills that are designated as urgent by the Federal Government are debated by the Bundestag and Bundesrat in a joint session without delay.[125] If a bill requires the consent of the Bundesrat, a majority is required for the bill to become law.[126]

---

[121] *Id.*

[122] *Id.* art. 113, para. 2.

[123] According to article 115a, paragraph 1 of the Basic Law, a "state of defense" exists if there is a "determination that the federal territory is under attack by armed force or imminently threatened with such an attack."

[124] *Id.* art. 115d.

[125] *Id.* art. 115d, para. 2, sentence 2.

[126] *Id.* art. 115d, para. 2, sentence 3.

Japan

Sayuri Umeda
Foreign Law Specialist

SUMMARY The current Diet of Japan was established in 1946 after the Second World War. Under the post-war Constitution, the Diet was designated the highest organ of state power and the sole law-making organ of the state.

The Diet consists of the House of Representatives and the House of Councillors. Under Japan's parliamentary cabinet system, the Prime Minister is the head of the Executive and elected from among Diet members.

Elections for the House of Representative are held every four years unless the House is dissolved. Elections for half of the House of Councillors are held every three years.

Bills are generally submitted to the House of Representatives before the House of Councillors. When both houses pass a bill, the bill is usually enacted into law.

I. Background

The Imperial Diet, Japan's first modern legislature, was established in 1890 under the 1889 Meiji Constitution, the first modern Constitution enacted in Japan.[1] The Meiji Constitution gave the Emperor a broad range of strong powers.[2] The Imperial Diet consisted of two houses: the House of Peers and the House of Representatives. The former drew its members from the Imperial Family, the Peers (other nobles), people who paid high taxes, and others appointed by the Emperor. The members of the latter were elected by limited franchise.[3]

The current Constitution was promulgated after the Second World War on November 3, 1946, and went into effect on May 3, 1947.[4] The Imperial Diet enacted election laws that would comply with the new Constitution before it became effective.[5] The 1945 amendment to the

---

[1] *The Promulgation of the Meiji Constitution and Educatron* [sic], MINISTRY OF EDUCATION, CULTURE, SPORTS, SCIENCE AND TECHNOLOGY, http://www.mext.go.jp/b_menu/hakusho/html/others/detail/1317324_htm (last visited Dec. 4, 2015), *archived at* https://perma.cc/TT6K-WGHJ.

[2] 9. 大日本帝国憲法の発布 [*Promulgation of Great Japan Imperial Constitution*], NATIONAL ARCHIVES OF JAPAN, http://www.archives.go.jp/exhibition/digital/modean_state/contents/constitutional-law/index.html (last visited Dec. 4, 2015), *archived at* https://perma.cc/JVV5-JA4B.

[3] *From Imperial Diet to National Diet*, HOUSE OF REPRESENTATIVES, http://www.shugiin.go.jp/internet/itdb_english.nsf/html/statics/guide/imperial.htm (last visited Dec. 4, 2015), *archived at* https://perma.cc/359V-2Y38.

[4] CONSTITUTION OF JAPAN (1946), translation available on Prime Minister and His Cabinet's website *at* http://japan.kantei.go.jp/constitution_and_government_of_japan/constitution_e_html, *archived at* https://perma.cc/D2PP-FT57.

[5] 衆議院議員選挙法中ヲ改正ス [*Amending House of Representatives Election Act*], NATIONAL ARCHIVES OF JAPAN, http://www.archives.go.jp/ayumi/kobetsu/s20_1945_06_html (last visited Dec. 4, 2015), *archived at*

House of Representatives Members Election Act gave women voting rights for the first time.[6] The first elections for both houses under the new Constitution were held on April 20 and 25, 1946.[7] When the new Constitution took effect, the Imperial Diet was dissolved, and a new Diet was born.[8] The first session of the National Diet was convened on May 20, 1947.[9]

Under the new Constitution, the Emperor lost his powers and became a "symbol" of the nation.[10] Instead, the Diet became the highest organ of state power.[11]

The Diet building is located in Nagatacho, Tokyo. The Prime Minister's residence is also located in Nagatacho. Therefore, "Nagatacho" is often used to refer to Japan's national government.[12] The Diet building was constructed for the Imperial Diet, and it was first used in December 1936 (during the 70th Session of the Imperial Diet). Japan's House of Representatives is located on the left side of the building, and the House of Councillors is located on the right.[13]

II. Constitutional Status and Role

The Diet, which consists of the House of Representatives and House of Councillors, is the sole law-making organ of the State.[14] Executive power is vested in the Cabinet.[15] The Prime Minister represents the Cabinet, submits bills, reports on general national affairs and foreign relations to the Diet, and exercises control and supervision over various administrative entities.[16]

---

https://perma.cc/KJ2Z-AHYE; House of Councillors Member Election Act, Act No. 11 of 1947, *abolished by* Act on Implementation of House of Councillors Act and Reorganization of Related Acts, Act No. 101 of 1950, art. 1.

[6] NATIONAL ARCHIVES OF JAPAN, *supra* note 5.

[7] 詳細年表 5, 1946 年 12 月 1 日～1947 年 6 月 23 日 [*Detailed Chronology 5 December 1, 1956–June 23, 1947*], NATIONAL DIET LIBRARY, http://www.ndl.go.jp/constitution/etc/history05.html (last visited Dec. 4, 2015), *archived at* https://perma.cc/QB4J-MT97.

[8] 皇室令及附属法令廃止ノ件 [Regarding Abolishment of Imperial House Order and Related Laws and Regulations], Imperial House Order No. 12 of 1947, *available at* http://www.geocities.jp/nakanolib/kou/ks22-12.htm, *archived at* https://perma.cc/32XT-LXDM (click "Uploaded page").

[9] *The National Diet*, HOUSE OF REPRESENTATIVES, http://www.shugiin.go.jp/internet/itdb_english.nsf/html/statics/guide/dietfun.htm (last visited Dec. 4, 2015), *archived at* https://perma.cc/8MM7-HWHE.

[10] CONSTITUTION arts. 1 and 4.

[11] *Id.* art. 41.

[12] John Spacey, *4 Things to Do in Nagatacho*, JAPAN TALK (Sept. 6, 2014), http://www.japan-talk.com/jt/new/nagatacho-in-tokyo, *archived at* https://perma.cc/HMB2-73DL.

[13] *Diet Building Facilities*, HOUSE OF REPRESENTATIVES, http://www.shugiin.go.jp/internet/itdb_english.nsf/html/statics/guide/bldg.htm (last visited Dec. 4, 2015), *archived at* https://perma.cc/KYS7-932S.

[14] CONSTITUTION arts. 41–42.

[15] *Id.* art. 65.

[16] *Id.* art. 72.

Under Japan's parliamentary cabinet system,[17] the Prime Minister is designated from among the members of the Diet by a resolution of the Diet.[18] The Cabinet is collectively responsible to the Diet in the exercise of executive power.[19] If the House of Representatives passes a no-confidence resolution, either the House of Representatives must be dissolved or the Cabinet must resign *en masse*.[20]

The Diet's powers, which are jointly exercised by its two houses, include the following:

1. Enactment of laws,
2. Decisions regarding the budget and other matters related to national finances,
3. Decisions regarding approval for the conclusion of international treaties, [and]
4. Designation of the Prime Minister . . . .[21]

In the rare event that the House of Councillors rejects a bill passed by the House of Representatives, the bill becomes law if passed again by the House of Representatives in a two-thirds vote.[22]

Chapter 1 of the Constitution contains provisions on the Emperor and his powers. However, as the Constitution states only that the Emperor is "the symbol of the State,"[23] there is controversy over whether Japan can be considered a constitutional monarchy and whether the Emperor is the actual head of state.[24]

III. Structure and Composition

The Diet's House of Representatives has 475 members, consisting of 295 members who are elected from single-seat districts and 180 proportionally elected from multiseat districts. The House of Councillors has 242 members, consisting of 146 elected from multiseat prefectures and ninety-six proportionally elected from multiseat constituencies.[25] The term of office for House

---

[17] *Parliamentary Cabinet System*, HOUSE OF REPRESENTATIVES, http://www.shugiin.go.jp/internet/itdb english nsf/html/statics/guide/parliamentary htm (last visited Dec. 8, 2015), *archived at* https://perma.cc/T86Z-RTTS.

[18] CONSTITUTION art. 67, para. 1.

[19] *Id*. art. 66, para. 3.

[20] *Id*. art. 69.

[21] *Powers of the National Diet*, HOUSE OF REPRESENTATIVES, http://www.shugiin.go.jp/internet/itdb english nsf/html/statics/guide/powers htm (last visited Dec. 8, 2015), *archived at* https://perma.cc/X4NN-V3CC.

[22] *Id.*; *Essay Comparing the Japanese and American Electoral Systems, in The Government of Modern Japan: Elections,* ASIA FOR EDUCATORS, COLUMBIA UNIVERSITY (2009), http://afe.easia.columbia.edu/special/japan 1900 elections.htm, *archived at* https://perma.cc/3253-JLDY.

[23] CONSTITUTION art. 1.

[24] 天皇と国民の憲法　「元首」と定め地位明確に [*Emperor and People's Constitution, Make the Position Clear by Stating "Head of State"*], SANKEI NEWSPAPER (Apr. 27, 2013), http://www.sankei.com/politics/news/130427/plt1304270013-n2 html, *archived at* https://perma.cc/NQ8Y-5WPY.

[25] Public Offices Election Act, Act No. 100 of 1950, *amended by* Act No. 60 of 2015, art. 4; ASIA FOR EDUCATORS, *supra* note 22; 衆議院小選挙区の区割りの改定等について [*Regarding Amendment of Allocation of Small*

of Representatives members is four years unless the House is dissolved within the term.[26] The term of office for the House of Councillors is six years, with half of the members elected every three years.[27] While citizens must be twenty-five years of age or older to run for office in the House of Representatives, the age requirement is thirty years of age or older for the House of Councillors.[28]

Each house has a Chairman and a Vice-chairman,[29] who remain in their positions for the extent of their terms as House members.[30] Chairmen are responsible for maintaining order in the house, managing meetings, supervising the administration of the house, and representing the house.[31]

The House of Representatives and the House of Councillors each have seventeen standing committees,[32] such as the Cabinet, Internal Affairs and Communications, Judicial Affairs, Foreign Affairs, and Financial Affairs committees.[33] Each house can pass resolutions to establish special committees for a given Diet session whenever necessary. Every Diet member serves on at least one standing committee during his or her term of office.[34]

The Liberal Democratic Party (LDP) has been Japan's most popular political party and has governed Japan most of the time since 1955.[35] The Democratic Party controlled the Diet and the Cabinet between 2009 and 2012, but had lost popularity by the end of 2011,[36] allowing the LDP

Election Districts], MINISTRY OF INTERNAL AFFAIRS AND COMMUNICATION (June 28, 2013), http://www.soumu. go.jp/senkyo/senkyo_s/news/senkyo/shu_kuwari/index.html, *archived at* https://perma.cc/PV2Y-2ZD2; 衆議院比例 代表選挙の選挙区（ブロック）と各選挙区別定数 [*House of Representatives Proportional Representation Districts (Blocks) and Number of Seats in Each District*] (map), MINISTRY OF INTERNAL AFFAIRS AND COMMUNICATION (June 25, 2000), http://www.soumu.go.jp/senkyo/senkyo_s/news/senkyo/shu_teisu/pdf/map.pdf, *archived at* https://perma.cc/VG7E-APNM.

[26] CONSTITUTION art. 45.

[27] *Id.* art. 46.

[28] Public Offices Election Act art. 10.

[29] Diet Act, Act No. 79 of 1947, *amended by* Act No. 86 of 2014, art. 17.

[30] *Id.* art. 18.

[31] *Id.* art. 19.

[32] *Types of Committees*, HOUSE OF REPRESENTATIVES, http://www.shugiin.go.jp/internet/itdb_english.nsf/html/ statics/guide/types_htm (last visited Dec. 8, 2015), *archived at* https://perma.cc/F426-PTME.

[33] *Standing Committees*, HOUSE OF REPRESENTATIVES, http://www.shugiin.go.jp/internet/itdb_english. nsf/html/statics/guide/committees.html (last visited Dec. 8, 2015), *archived at* https://perma.cc/6XVG-7LKJ.

[34] *Types of Committees*, *supra* note 32.

[35] Jonathan Soble, *Portrait of Japan's Main Political Parties*, FINANCIAL TIMES (Dec. 16, 2012), http://www.ft. com/cms/s/0/9281ca7c-4742-11e2-a899-00144feab49a.html (by subscription).

[36] *Poll*, TV STATION, http://www.tv-asahi.co.jp/hst/poll/graph_seitou.html (last visited Dec. 8, 2015), *archived at* https://perma.cc/43TT-MMQW.

to return to power in the 2012 election.[37] Japan has several other parties,[38] including the Japanese Communist Party,[39] which has never held many seats in the Diet but still has a strong presence there.[40]

IV. Elections

Elections for the House of Representatives are held every four years unless the House is dissolved.[41] When it is dissolved, a general election is held within forty days from the date of dissolution.[42] Elections for half of the House of Councillors are held every three years.[43] There are no provisions in the Constitution or any Diet acts that impose term limits on Diet members.

The most recent Diet election was for the House of Representatives in December 2014, in which the LDP won a landslide victory.[44] The next House of Representatives election will be held in 2018, unless the House is dissolved earlier. The most recent House of Councillors election was in July 2013, and also resulted in a landslide victory for the LDP.[45] The next House of Councillors election will be held in the summer of 2016.

The voter turnout rate has been falling in recent years, hitting a record low of 52.66% in the 2014 House of Representatives election.[46] The highest percentage of voters are in their sixties, followed by voters in their fifties.[47]

---

[37] *UPDATE: Abe's LDP Dominates Election; Noda Resigns After DPJ Humiliation*, ASAHI SHIMBUN (Dec. 17, 2012), http://ajw.asahi.com/article/behind_news/politics/AJ201212170006, *archived at* https://perma.cc/G6F5-SGEU.

[38] *Political Parties*, JAPAN LINKS, http://web-japan.org/links/government/political/political.html (last visited Dec. 8, 2015), *archived at* https://perma.cc/9A72-829M.

[39] For more information, see the website of the Japanese Communist Party, http://www.jcp.or.jp/english/.

[40] Soble, *supra* note 35.

[41] CONSTITUTION art. 45.

[42] Public Offices Election Act art. 31, para. 1.

[43] CONSTITUTION art. 46.

[44] 自公が圧勝３２５議席…民主伸び悩み、維新苦戦 [*LDP-Komei Landslide Victory with 325 Seats . . . Democrats Failed to Gain More Seats, Innovation Had Hard Fight*], YOMIURI NEWSPAPER (Dec. 15, 2014), http://www.yomiuri.co.jp/election/shugiin/2014/news/20141215-OYT1T50011.html, *archived at* https://perma.cc/KW4E-DELF.

[45] 参院選 2013 [*House of Councillors Election 2013*], YOMIURI NEWSPAPER, http://www.yomiuri.co.jp/election/sangiin/2013, *archived at* https://perma.cc/M2W5-XD9Z (click on "Screen capture" tab).

[46] 国政選挙における投票率の推移 [*Changes of Voter Turnout Ratio in National Elections*], MINISTRY OF INTERNAL AFFAIRS AND COMMUNICATION, http://www.soumu.go.jp/senkyo/senkyo_s/news/sonota/ritu (last visited Dec. 8, 2015), *archived at* https://perma.cc/Y55R-B5Q9.

[47] 国政選挙における年代別投票率について [*Regarding Voter Turnout Ratio in National Elections by Age Groups*], MINISTRY OF INTERNAL AFFAIRS AND COMMUNICATION, http://www.soumu.go.jp/senkyo/senkyo_s/news/sonota/nendaibetu (last visited Dec. 8, 2015), *archived at* https://perma.cc/T6VL-QZGN.

V. Legislative Process

Legislation can be submitted by Diet members,[48] a Diet committee,[49] or the Cabinet.[50] When members of the House of Representatives submit a legislative bill, the bill must have the support of twenty or more members. In the case of the House of Councillors, the bill must be supported by ten or more members.[51] Legislative bills requiring the passage of a budget, however, must have the support of fifty of more members of the House of Representatives or twenty or more members of the House of Councillors.[52]

Bills are usually submitted to the House of Representatives first, but this is not always the case.[53] For example, at the beginning of a Diet session, the House of Councillors can receive bills first; otherwise, the House would have no bills to discuss until the House of Representatives passed a bill and sent it to the House of Councillors. Once a bill has been submitted to a house, the Chairman of that house refers the bill to the committee with jurisdiction over the bill.[54] After receiving a briefing on the bill from the members who submitted the bill or from the minister of state in charge, the committee members question the members who submitted the bill, the minister of state, or other government officials regarding the bill.[55] A vote is then taken in committee and the bill is sent to the plenary session, unless the committee decides that it is not necessary to do so.[56] Once a bill is passed by the plenary session of a house, it is sent to the other house.[57] When the other house also passes the bill, the bill becomes an act[58] and is sent to the Emperor through the Cabinet.[59] All ministers of state and the Prime Minister must sign the act.[60] The Emperor then promulgates the act within thirty days by publication in the official gazette.[61]

---

[48] Diet Act art. 56.

[49] *Id.* art. 50-2.

[50] Cabinet Act, Act No. 79 of 1947, *amended by* Act No. 86 of 2014.

[51] Diet Act art. 56, para. 1.

[52] *Id.*

[53] 参議院のあらまし [*Abstract of the House of Councillors*], HOUSE OF COUNCILLORS, http://www.sangiin.go.jp/japanese/aramashi/houritu html (last visited Dec. 8, 2015), *archived at* https://perma.cc/CKW9-2J9Y.

[54] Diet Act art. 56, para. 2.

[55] *Deliberation of Bills*, HOUSE OF REPRESENTATIVES, http://www.shugiin.go.jp/internet/itdb english.nsf/html/statics/guide/deliberation htm (last visited Dec. 8, 2015), *archived at* https://perma.cc/K6D7-8C96.

[56] Diet Act art. 56, para. 2.

[57] *Id.* art. 83.

[58] CONSTITUTION art. 59, para. 1.

[59] Diet Act art. 65, para. 1.

[60] CONSTITUTION art. 74.

[61] *Id.* art. 7, item 1; Diet Act art. 66. Promulgation by official gazette is a custom. Minori Iba, 官報 [*Official Gazette*], RIPPO TO CHOSA, No. 318 (July 2011), available on Legislative Bureau, House of Councillors' website, *at* http://houseikyoku.sangiin.go.jp/column/column090 htm, *archived at* https://perma.cc/DA5S-4G2Q.

Regarding the national budget,[62] the Cabinet makes a budget and submits it to the Diet for its decision.[63]   The House of Representatives makes a decision on it first.   If the House of Councillors' decision on the budget differs from that of the House of Representatives and no agreement can be reached in a joint committee of both houses, or if the House of Councillors fails to take final action within thirty days after receiving the budget passed by the House of Representatives, the decision of the House of Representatives stands as the decision of the Diet.[64]

When the Cabinet submits a treaty for approval to the Diet,[65] the approval process is the same as for a budget—it is sent to the House of Representatives first, and the House of Representatives has control over the final decision .[66]

---

[62] CONSTITUTION art. 86.

[63] *Id.* art. 73.

[64] *Id.* art. 60.

[65] *Id.* art. 73.

[66] *Id.* art. 61.

Mexico

Gustavo Guerra
Senior Foreign Law Specialist

SUMMARY   Mexico's Congress was established in 1917 and has two chambers: the Chamber of Representatives and the Chamber of Senators (which is commonly referred to as the Republic's Senate). The Chamber of Representatives is comprised of five hundred members who are elected every three years, with the possibility of being elected for up to four consecutive terms. The Chamber of Senators is comprised of 128 senators elected every six years, with the possibility of being elected for up to two consecutive terms. Mexico is a federal republic formed by thirty-two sovereign states united in a federation as provided by the Mexican Constitution. The Constitution provides an extensive list of powers reserved for Congress. The legislative process requires both chambers of Congress to agree on the text of a bill, both in general and article by article. Both chambers of Mexico's Congress have committees aimed at overseeing, researching, and generally assisting Congress in the fulfillment of its duties concerning a number of specific topics.

I. Background

A. Establishment of the Federal Congress

Mexico's Congress was established in 1917 by the Constitution enacted that year, which is still in force.[1] Previous Constitutions in force in Mexico during the nineteenth century also provided for the existence of a national legislature. Specifically, Mexico's 1824 Constitution stated that federal legislative power was to be exercised by a General Congress comprised of two chambers, one of representatives and another of senators.[2]

In 1857, another Constitution was enacted, which provided that the legislature would be comprised of only one chamber of representatives.[3] However, in 1874 this Constitution was amended in order to reinstate the Senate based on the argument that in a federal republic such as Mexico, it was necessary to have a bicameral congressional system comprising representatives of states as a whole (i.e., senators) as well as representatives from specific districts.[4]

---

[1] CONSTITUCIÓN POLÍTICA DE LOS ESTADOS UNIDOS MEXICANOS [POLITICAL CONSTITUTION OF THE UNITED MEXICAN STATES, HEREINAFTER "CONST."] art. 50, DIARIO OFICIAL DE LA FEDERACIÓN [D.O.], Feb. 5, 1917, available *as amended through* July 2015 on the website of Mexico's House of Representatives, *at* http://www.diputados.gob.mx/Leyes Biblio/pdf/1_100715.pdf, *archived at* https://perma.cc/TF29-795A.

[2] *El Senado Mexicano, Breve Historia* [*Brief History of the Mexican Senate*], CAMARA DE SENADORES [CHAMBER OF SENATORS], http://www.senado.gob.mx/index.php?ver=sen&mn=1&sm=3 (last visited Jan. 15, 2016), *archived at* https://perma.cc/5KQ4-WSR2.

[3] *Id.*

[4] *Id.*

B. Location of Congress

Mexico's Federal District (best known as Mexico City) is the nation's capital and the place where Congress is located.[5]

Mexico's 1824 Constitution stated that Congress had the authority to select the location in which the federal legislative branch would reside.[6] Pursuant to this authority, Congress chose Mexico City as its location, as this was the country's focal point for a wide variety of activities, including business, politics, economics and cultural affairs.[7]

The legislative chambers are located in Mexico City's Historic District.[8] The location of the building of the Chamber of Representatives was chosen due to its close proximity to Mexico's National Palace (i.e., the President's office building).[9] This Chamber was built with a central section that houses a main hall where the Representatives meet for their sessions.[10] This hall is surrounded by a number of wings that house individual representative offices, committees, and administrative offices.[11] The façade of the building was built with materials that reflect the three national colors (green, white and red).[12] The Senate occupies a two-story building which has a central courtyard and houses a wide variety of paintings and sculptures that illustrate key figures and events of Mexico's history.[13]

---

[5] CONST. arts. 44, 49, 50.

[6] CONSTITUCIÓN FEDERAL DE LOS ESTADOS UNIDOS MEXICANOS [FEDERAL CONSTITUTION OF THE UNITED MEXICAN STATES] art. 50 (XXVIII), Oct. 4, 1824, available as originally enacted on the website of Mexico's House of Representatives, *at* http://www.diputados.gob.mx/biblioteca/bibdig/const_mex/const_1824.pdf, *archived at* https://perma.cc/4RZ3-WSYE.

[7] 2 MIGUEL CARBONELL ET AL., CONSTITUCIÓN POLÍTICA DE LOS ESTADOS UNIDOS MEXICANOS: COMENTADA Y CONCORDADA [POLITICAL CONSTITUTION OF THE UNITED MEXICAN STATES ANNOTATED] art. 44, at 141–42 (15th ed. 2000).

[8] EDNA BARBA ET AL., EL PALACIO LEGISLATIVO DE SAN LÁZARO – SEDE DE LA CÁMARA DE DIPUTADOS 79 (2003), available on the website of Mexico's House of Representatives, *at* http://www.diputados.gob.mx/sedia/biblio/virtual/dip/pal_legis/pal_legisla.pdf, *archived at* https://perma.cc/C6GZ-LQZV. *See also El Senado Mexicano, Sede Histórica [History of the Senate's location]*, CAMARA DE SENADORES [CHAMBER OF SENATORS], http://www.senado.gob.mx/index.php?ver=sen&mn=1&sm=7 (last visited Jan. 21, 2016), *archived at* https://perma.cc/7SZM-4Y8Q.

[9] EDNA BARBA ET AL, *supra* note 8, at 79.

[10] *Id.* at 84.

[11] *Id.*

[12] *Id.* at 85.

[13] *El Senado Mexicano, Sede Histórica [History of the Senate's location]*, CAMARA DE SENADORES [CHAMBER OF SENATORS], http://www.senado.gob mx/index.php?ver=sen&mn=1&sm=7 (last visited Jan. 21, 2016), *archived at* https://perma.cc/7SZM-4Y8Q.

II. Constitutional Status and Role

A. Mexican System of Government

Mexico is a federal republic whose national government is comprised of the executive, legislative, and judicial branches.[14]

The country is formed by thirty-one states and a Federal District that are free and sovereign with respect to their respective territories but united in a federation as provided by the Mexican Constitution, which indicates that the powers that are not expressly granted by it to federal authorities are deemed reserved for the authorities of the Mexican states.[15]

Article 122 of the Mexican Constitution provides that the government of the Federal District is organized in a system in which both the federal government and the local Executive, Legislative and Judicial branches exercise certain powers, in a structure whose main features may be summarized as follows:

A. The (local) executive power is a "Chief of government," directly elected by the citizens of the Federal District;

B. The (local) legislative power is vested in a Legislative Assembly (whose members are also elected by the District's citizens), with power to pass legislation on matters that are expressly indicated in article 122 of the Constitution (such as legislating on local matters, including local transportation, tourism and lodging services);

C. The Magistrates of the (local) Superior Tribunal of the Federal District are designated by the Legislative Assembly, upon the proposal of the Chief of government;

D. The Federal District is … divided into *"Delegaciones"* (which are to some extent similar to boroughs), but those who head them are popularly and directly elected;

E. The (federal) Congress … has power to legislate on certain matters relating to the Federal District (such as legislating on matters of the District's public debt).[16]

The Mexican President heads the federal executive branch and has broad executive powers, including the authority to direct foreign policy and to command Mexico's armed forces.[17]

B. Legislative Role of the Congress Under the Constitution

Mexico's Constitution provides that Congress constitutes the country's federal legislative branch, which is comprised of the Chamber of Representatives and the Chamber of Senators.[18]

---

[14] CONST. arts. 40, 49.

[15] *Id.* arts. 40, 41, 43, 124. Note that as of late January 2016, the Federal District is in the process of becoming a state entity pursuant to a constitutional amendment to that effect, which is expected to be published and enacted by Mexico's President later this year. Details concerning the implementation of such constitutional amendment are expected to become available after the amendment is enacted.

[16] JOSÉ MARÍA SERNA DE LA GARZA, THE CONSTITUTION OF MEXICO: A CONTEXTUAL ANALYSIS 156, 157 (2013). *See also* CONST. art. 122.

[17] CONST. arts. 80, 89, 90.

Article 73 of the Mexican Constitution provides an extensive list of powers reserved for Congress, including the following:

- Admitting new states to the country

- Issuing declarations of war, in view of information presented by the President

- Imposing taxes necessary to cover the nation's budget

- Preventing the restriction of commerce between the states

- Passing laws on a wide variety of areas, including nationality, the legal status of foreigners, citizenship, naturalization, immigration, and national security[19]

III. Structure and Composition

A. House and Senate Membership

Mexico's Chamber of Representatives is comprised of five hundred representatives, three hundred of whom represent a federal electoral district. The other two hundred are chosen through proportional representation, a complex system whereby political parties that fulfill certain requirements are allowed to nominate candidates to these seats, which are assigned based on the proportion of votes obtained in an election by such parties.[20]

The Chamber of Senators (which is commonly referred to as the Republic's Senate) has 128 senators, ninety-six of whom are elected in the thirty-two Mexican states (three senators per state), and thirty-two of whom are chosen by proportional representation, i.e., these seats are assigned based on the proportion of votes obtained by political parties in a nationwide election.[21]

The two chambers of Congress are elected under the rules discussed in Part IV of this report.

B. Political Parties

Currently, there are three main political parties represented in Mexico's Chamber of Representatives: the Institutional Revolutionary Party, the National Action Party, and the Party of the Democratic Revolution.[22] In addition, five other minor political parties are represented and two representatives have no party affiliation.[23] Seats in the Chamber of Representatives are distributed by political parties as follows:

---

[18] *Id.* art. 50.

[19] *Id.* art. 73.

[20] *Id.* arts. 52–54.

[21] *Id.* art. 56. *See also* Ley General de Instituciones y Procedimientos Electorales, art. 14, D.O., May 23, 2014, available as originally enacted on the website of Mexico's Chamber of Representatives, *at* http://www.diputados. gob.mx/LeyesBiblio/pdf/LGIPE_130815.pdf, *archived at* https://perma.cc/W75Q-SCLP.

[22] *Total de Diputados por Partido Politico* [*Representatives by Political Parties*], CAMARA DE DIPUTADOS [CHAMBER OF REPRESENTATIVES], http://www.diputados.gob mx/apps/gps_parlam htm (last visited Jan. 15, 2016).

[23] *Id.*

- Institutional Revolutionary Party: 207

- National Action Party: 109

- Party of the Democratic Revolution: 60

- Ecologist Green Party: 42

- National Regeneration Movement: 35

- Citizen Movement Party: 25

- New Alliance Party: 11

- Social Compact Party: 8

- Independent Party: 2.[24]

As of October 2015, seats in the Mexican Senate were allocated by political party as follows:

- Institutional Revolutionary Party: 52

- National Action Party: 37

- Party of the Democratic Revolution: 21

- Ecologist Green Party: 7

- Labor Party: 6

- New Alliance Party: 1

- Independent Party: 1[25]

C. Role of the President of the Chamber of Representatives and other Salient Leadership Roles

The President of the Chamber of Representatives conducts institutional relations with the Chamber of Senators as well as with the other branches of the federal government and state authorities, and is the Chamber's representative in matters of parliamentary diplomacy.[26] Among other duties, the President of the Chamber also

---

[24] *Id.*

[25] *Senadores por Grupo Parlamentario [Senators by Political Parties]*, CAMARA DE SENADORES [CHAMBER OF SENATORS], http://www.senado.gob.mx/index.php?ver=int&mn=4&sm=5 (last visited Jan. 15, 2016), *archived at* https://perma.cc/K22J-2CRU.

[26] Ley Orgánica del Congreso General de los Estados Unidos Mexicanos [Organic Law of the General Congress of the Mexican United States] art. 22, D.O., Sept. 3, 1999, available *as amended through* May 2015 on the website of Mexico's Chamber of Representatives, *at* http://www.diputados.gob.mx/LeyesBiblio/pdf/168_180515.pdf, *archived at* https://perma.cc/D4W3-XGX9.

- presides over the Chamber's sessions;

- signs legislation and resolutions passed by Congress, in conjunction with the Senate's leadership;

- legally represents the Chamber and has the authority to delegate this duty as necessary; and

- signs the Chamber's correspondence and other communications.[27]

The President of the Chamber of Representatives is assisted in his/her duties by three Vice-Presidents of the chamber, who may be assigned by the President to represent the Chamber as necessary at protocol events.[28]

The President and Vice-Presidents are elected by the members of the Chamber.[29]

D. Role of the President of the Senate and other Salient Leadership Roles

Similarly, members of the Mexican Senate also elect a President and three Vice-Presidents who assist the former in the discharge of his/her duties and substitute for him/her during temporary absences.[30] The President of the Senate has broad powers over the Chamber's operations, providing legal representation and signing laws passed by Congress in conjunction with the Chamber of Representatives' leadership.[31]

E. Parliamentary Committees

Both chambers of Mexico's Congress have committees aimed at overseeing, researching, and generally assisting Congress in the fulfillment of its duties concerning a number of specific topics.[32]

Specifically, the Chamber of Representatives currently has the following fifty-two committees: agriculture; drinking water; northern and southern border affairs; Indian affairs; immigration; vulnerable groups; climate change; science and technology; competitiveness; communications; culture and cinematography; national defense, sports; rights of children; human rights; metropolitan development; municipal development; rural development; social development; urban development; economy; education; energy; social economy; federalism; cattle industry; governance; treasury; gender equality; infrastructure; justice; youth; navy; environment; fishing; population; budget; emergency management; constitutional matters; radio and television;

---

[27] *Id.* arts. 22, 23.

[28] *Id.* arts. 17-1, 24.

[29] *Id.* art. 17.

[30] *Id.* arts. 62, 67, 69.

[31] *Id.* art. 67.

[32] *Id.* arts. 39, 45, 85, 90, 98.

hydraulic resources; agrarian reform; foreign relations; health; public safety; social security; labor; transparency and anticorruption; transportation; tourism; and housing.[33]

The Senate currently has the following thirty committees: administration; agriculture, cattle industry and rural development; Indian affairs; library and editorial matters; commerce; communications and transportation; national defense; human rights; social development; federal district; education, culture, science, and technology; energy; legislative studies; federalism and municipal development; governance; treasury; judicial matters; justice; navy; Belisario Dominguez medal; environment, natural resources, and fishing; gender equality; constitutional matters; agrarian reform; regulations and parliamentary practices; foreign relations; health and social security; public safety; labor; and tourism.[34]

Special committees may be formed by either chamber as Representatives and Senators see fit in order to address a particular issue.[35]

IV. Elections

Federal elections are organized and managed by Mexico's National Elections Institute.[36] The most recent federal election was held on June 7, 2015, and the next federal election will take place on July 1, 2018.[37] Voter turnout for the 2015 election was 47%.[38]

As stated above, Mexico's Chamber of Representatives is comprised of five hundred representatives (elected every three years, with the possibility of being elected for up to four consecutive terms), three hundred of whom are elected by a relative majority and represent an individual federal electoral district.[39] The other two hundred representatives obtain their seats by proportional representation.[40]

In terms of population represented, the federal electoral districts are determined by dividing the total number of Mexico's inhabitants by three hundred (i.e., the number of districts).[41] Allocation of the federal electoral districts among the Mexican states is done pursuant to data

---

[33] *Id.* art. 39.

[34] *Id.* art. 90.

[35] *Id.* arts. 42, 85.

[36] CONST. art. 41-V.

[37] Ley General de Instituciones y Procedimientos Electorales, transitory arts. 9th and 11th, D.O., May 23, 2014, available as originally enacted on the website of Mexico's Chamber of Representatives, *at* http://www.diputados.gob.mx/LeyesBiblio/pdf/LGIPE_130815.pdf, *archived at* https://perma.cc/W75Q-SCLP.

[38] *Participacion ciudadana* [*Voter Turnout*], INSTITUTO NACIONAL ELECTORAL [MEXICO'S NATIONAL ELECTION INSTITUTE], http://prep2015.ine mx/Nacional/VotosPorPartido (last visited Jan. 15, 2016), *archived at* https://perma.cc/46TG-LYPA (click "See the Screenshot View").

[39] CONST. arts. 51–53, 59.

[40] *Id.* art. 54.

[41] *Id.* art. 53.

obtained in the most recent population census, although each state must have at least two federal representatives.[42]

The Chamber of Senators is comprised of 128 senators (elected every six years, with the possibility of being elected for up to two consecutive terms), of whom ninety-six are elected in the thirty-two Mexican states (three senators per state), and thirty-two chosen by proportional representation.[43]

V. Legislative Process

The Mexican Constitution provides guidelines concerning the legislative process applicable to a standard bill, which have been summarized as follows:

> According to article 71 of the Constitution, the power to introduce bills for consideration is vested in: the president of the Republic; (representatives) and senators of the federal Congress; State legislatures; and a number of citizens that is equivalent to no less than 0.13 per cent of registered voters. Moreover, it has to be noticed that the president of the Republic has the exclusive power to introduce bills that refer to federal income and budget of each year.
>
> . . . .
>
> With respect to (representatives) and senators, the Constitution does not foresee a specific number of legislators required to exercise the power to introduce bills; therefore, it is understood that this can be done either by individual legislators or groups of them. (...) State legislatures also have power to introduce bills in the general Congress, but in practice they do not do so often.
>
> The rules on the relationship between the Chamber of (representatives) and the Senate in the context of the legislative process can be found in article 72 of the Constitution. Essentially, both chambers of Congress must agree on the text of a bill, both in general and article-by-article, in order to refer it to the president of the Republic (who shall either promulgate the new statute or veto the bill).[44]

Generally, bills may be introduced in either of the two chambers, but bills that deal with certain debt matters (*empréstitos*), taxes, or recruitment of troops must first be introduced and discussed in the Chamber of Representatives.[45]

A brief summary of the steps that standard bills go through from introduction in one of the legislative chambers (the chamber of origin of the bill) to approval by the other chamber (the reviewing chamber) follows:

---

[42] *Id.*

[43] *Id.* arts. 56, 59.

[44] JOSÉ MARÍA SERNA DE LA GARZA, *supra* note 16, at 62, 63.

[45] CONST. art. 72-H.

- **Introduction:** Any bill introduced must first be submitted for review to the committee that has jurisdiction over the bill's topic.

- **Review and Approval by Committees:** A report on the bill's particulars is prepared for the consideration of the members of the committee, and if they approve the bill, it is then referred for consideration by the rest of the members of the chamber.

- **Discussion:** The bill is discussed by the full chamber, both in general and in particular (article by article).

- **Vote:** The bill is then subject to a vote and, if approved, it is submitted to the other chamber (the reviewing chamber), which in turn follows the same procedure (review and approval by the appropriate committee, and discussion and vote by the full chamber). The reviewing chamber may approve the bill, or it may propose changes and return the bill to the chamber of origin for further discussion.[46]

- **Promulgation:** As stated above, "both chambers of Congress must agree on the text of a bill, both in general and article-by-article, in order to refer it to the president of the Republic (who shall either promulgate the new statute or veto the bill)."[47]

---

[46] *Proceso Legislativo* [*Legislative Process*], CAMARA DE SENADORES [CHAMBER OF SENATORS], http://www.senado.gob.mx/index.php?ver=sen&mn=1&sm=2 (last updated Nov. 2015), *archived at* https://perma.cc/VB5C-LEAM.

[47] JOSÉ MARÍA SERNA DE LA GARZA, *supra* note 16, at 63.

South Korea[*]

Sayuri Umeda
Foreign Law Specialist

SUMMARY   Korea's National Assembly was established on May 31, 1948. On August 15, 1948, the Republic of Korea (South Korea) was proclaimed. The National Assembly building has been located in Yeouido, Seoul since 1975.

    South Korea is a democratic republic with a presidential system of government. In addition to its legislative power, the National Assembly decides upon budget bills submitted by the Executive. The National Assembly also consents to the conclusion of treaties and declarations of war.

    The National Assembly may recommend the removal of the Prime Minister or a state council member from office. The National Assembly may also pass motions for the impeachment of the President and other officials and justices.

    The National Assembly is unicameral and has three hundred members. The next election will be held in 2016. In the last election in 2012, two major parties competed for the majority of seats, but many small parties are also represented.

    Bills are sent to relevant committees after introduction. If the committee does not repeal the bill, it is sent to the plenary session. In some cases, a bill may be sent to another committee before the plenary session. When the bill is passed by the plenary session, it is sent to the President for promulgation.

I. Background

A. Establishment of South Korean Government After World War II

After World War II the Allied Powers temporarily divided Korea along the thirty-eighth parallel between north and south. North Korea soon became a Communist state under the influence of the Soviet Union.[1] In the south, the United States military governed the area. To establish an independent government, the United Nations Temporary Commission on Korea was formed to assist and supervise the first election of a national assembly. Constitutional Assembly elections were held on May 10, 1948. The National Assembly was established on May 31, 1948. The

---

[*] At present there are no Law Library of Congress research staff members versed in Korean. This report has been prepared by the author's reliance on practiced legal research methods and on the basis of relevant legal resources, chiefly in English, currently available in the Law Library and online.

[1] *Hidden Korea*, PUBLIC BROADCASTING SERVICE, http://www.pbs.org/hiddenkorea/history.htm (last visited Dec. 7, 2015), *archived at* https://perma.cc/WLC6-K7JJ.

National Assembly adopted a Constitution[2] that established a presidential form of government. On August 15, 1948, the Republic of Korea (South Korea) was proclaimed.[3]

The first Constitution was amended in 1952 and 1954, and succeeded by new versions in 1960, 1963, 1972, 1980, and 1987. The 1963 Constitution was amended in 1969. Constitutions were disregarded with varying degrees by South Korea's presidents. Until Kim Yongsam's presidency (1993–1997), South Korea had frequently been described as a dictatorship or military dictatorship. Recognition of constitutional obligations began under the presidency of Roh Tae Woo (1988–1993) and continued under Kim Yongsam.[4]

B. Political Parties

It appears that political parties have short lives. Some two hundred political parties have formed since World War II.[5] One scholar described the situation as follows: "[political parties] may sprout, but few grow, most shortly wither, and only the exceptions flourish for a season or two, but then are transmogrified into a new incarnations and names."[6] Political leaders do not emerge through parties. As explained by another scholar, "[t]he leader does not represent the party: rather it is the other way around; the party constitutes the leader's support network."[7]

C. Building

The National Assembly building is located in Yeouido, Seoul. It did not have its own building for the first twenty-five years. In 1948, the Constituent Assembly opened in the conference room of the former City Hall in Seoul. After the Korean War broke out, the Assembly held sessions in provisional chambers, moving around southern cities such as Daegu and Busan. The Assembly later returned to the annex building of the City Hall in Seoul. The construction of a new National Assembly building finally began in 1969, was completed in August 1975, and officially dedicated to the National Assembly on September 2, 1975.[8]

---

[2] CONSTITUTION OF THE REPUBLIC OF KOREA, July 17, 1948.

[3] *South Korea Under United States Occupation, 1945–48, in* FEDERAL RESEARCH DIVISION, LIBRARY OF CONGRESS, SOUTH KOREA: A COUNTRY STUDY (Andrea Matles Savada & William Shaw eds., 1990), http://countrystudies. us/south-korea/9 htm (last visited Dec. 7, 2015), *archived at* https://perma.cc/WKU5-RT37.

[4] Keith Pratt & Richard Rutt, *Constitution, (2) South Korea, in* KOREA: A HISTORICAL AND CULTURAL DICTIONARY 90 (2013).

[5] David I. Steinberg & Myung Shin, *From Entourage to Ideology? Tensions in South Korean Political Parties in Transition* 2 (East-West Center Working Papers, Politics, Governance, and Security Series, No. 9, Aug. 2005), http://www.eastwestcenter.org/system/tdf/private/PSwp009.pdf?file=1&type=node&id=32081, *archived at* https://perma.cc/TRJ9-UJKQ. Parties are listed on the National Assembly's website, at http://korea.assembly. go kr/int/past 03.jsp (last visited Dec. 9, 2015), *archived at* https://perma.cc/P8MH-Y9NH.

[6] *Id.* at 1.

[7] Geir Helgesen, *Democracy in South Korea* 28, 35 (Nordic Institute of Asian Studies [NIAS] Reports No. 18, revised ed. 1995), *quoted in* Steinburg & Shin, *supra* note 5, at 1.

[8] *NA Building in the Past*, NATIONAL ASSEMBLY, http://korea.assembly.go kr/int/past 05.jsp (last visited Dec. 7, 2015), *archived at* https://perma.cc/XL3C-LH37.

II. Constitutional Status and Role

The current 1987 Constitution declares South Korea a democratic republic[9] and establishes a presidential system.[10] The President, who is elected by nationwide direct ballot, is the head of state[11] and serves a single five-year term.[12] The President appoints public officials, including the Prime Minister and heads of executive agencies.[13] The President performs his executive functions through the State Council, which is made up of fifteen to thirty members, including the President and Prime Minister.[14] The appointment of the Prime Minister must be approved by the National Assembly.[15] Other members of the State Council are appointed by the President upon recommendation of the Prime Minister.[16]

The Constitution vests legislative power in the National Assembly.[17] The President may attend and address the National Assembly or express his views by written message.[18] The National Assembly also deliberates and decides upon the national budget bill.[19] When the Executive plans to issue national bonds or to conclude contracts that may incur financial obligations on the state outside of the budget, it must have the prior concurrence of the National Assembly.[20] Further, the National Assembly gives its consent to the conclusion and ratification of treaties, declarations of war, the dispatch of armed forces to foreign states, and the stationing of alien forces in the territory of South Korea.[21]

The National Assembly may also pass a recommendation for the removal of the Prime Minister or a state council member from office. Such a recommendation for removal may be introduced by one-third or more of the total members of the National Assembly, and must be passed with the concurrent vote of a majority of the total members of the National Assembly.[22] Further, in cases where the President, Prime Minister, members of the State Council, heads of executive ministries, judges, or other public officials have violated the Constitution or other acts in the

---

[9] CONSTITUTION OF REPUBLIC OF KOREA art. 1(1), Constitution No. 10, Oct. 29, 1987, *translated in* STATUTES OF THE REPUBLIC OF KOREA, http://elaw.klri re.kr/eng_service/lawView.do?hseq=1&lang=ENG, *archived at* https://perma.cc/XHC5-R2EJ.

[10] *Id.* art. 66.

[11] *Id.* arts. 66(1) & 67(1).

[12] *Id.* art. 70.

[13] *Id.* arts. 78, 86(1), 87(1), 94, 98(2), 104 (1)(2).

[14] *Id.* arts. 87, 88.

[15] *Id.* art. 86(1).

[16] *Id.* art. 87(1).

[17] *Id.* art. 40.

[18] *Id.* art. 81.

[19] *Id.* art. 54(1).

[20] *Id.* art. 58.

[21] *Id.* art. 60.

[22] *Id.* art. 63.

performance of their official duties, the National Assembly may pass motions for their impeachment.[23] A motion for the impeachment of the President may be proposed by a majority of the total members of the National Assembly but must be approved by two-thirds or more of the total members of the National Assembly. A motion for impeachment of other officials may be proposed by one-third or more of the total members of the National Assembly, and requires a concurrent vote of a majority of the total members of the National Assembly for passage.[24]

III. Structure and Composition

The National Assembly is unicameral. It is composed of three hundred publicly elected members.[25]

The Speaker of the National Assembly represents the National Assembly, regulates its proceedings, maintains order, and supervises its affairs.[26] The Speaker and Deputy-Speaker of the National Assembly are elected by the votes of a majority of all the members.[27] When a member is elected as the Speaker, he or she cannot be registered in any party from the day following the election and throughout his or her term of office.[28] The term of the Speaker and Deputy-Speaker is two years.[29]

There are sixteen standing committees in the National Assembly, including the House Steering Committee, the Legislation and Judiciary Committee, the National Policy Committee, and the Strategy and Finance Committee.[30] The National Assembly can also establish special committees, as necessary.[31]

IV. Elections

The term of office of members of the National Assembly is four years.[32] The last election for National Assembly members was held in 2012.[33] Therefore, the next election will be held in 2016.

---

[23] *Id.* art. 65(1).

[24] *Id.* art. 65(2).

[25] *Members*, NATIONAL ASSEMBLY, http://korea.assembly.go kr/int/org_03.jsp (last visited Dec. 7, 2015), *archived at* https://perma.cc/NG2E-356D.

[26] National Assembly Act, Act No. 5, Oct. 2, 1948, *amended by* Act No. 11453, May 25, 2012, art. 10, *translated in* STATUTES OF THE REPUBLIC OF KOREA, http://elaw klri.re kr/eng_service/lawView.do?hseq=25732&lang=ENG, *archived at* https://perma.cc/4MML-7VXU.

[27] *Id.* art. 15.

[28] *Id.* art. 20-2.

[29] *Id.* art. 9.

[30] *Committees*, NATIONAL ASSEMBLY, http://korea.assembly.go kr/int/org_06.jsp (last visited Dec. 7, 2015), *archived at* https://perma.cc/3FGD-YQGC.

[31] *Id.*

[32] CONSTITUTION art. 42.

The National Assembly is composed of three hundred members, 246 elected by a plurality of votes from electoral districts and fifty-four through a proportional representation system where seats are distributed to parties based on the percentage of total votes they garnered.[34]

In the 2012 election, voter turnout was 54.26%.[35] Two major parties competed in the election. The Saenuri Party won 152 seats out of three hundred, while the Democratic United Party won 127.[36] As in the previous several elections, around 30% of representatives in the National Assembly were first-time representatives in 2012.[37]

V. Legislative Process

Bills may be introduced by members of the National Assembly or by the Executive.[38] When National Assembly members propose a bill, the concurrence of ten or more National Assembly members is required.[39] Where a bill accompanying measures on budgets or funds is proposed by members or submitted by the Executive, a written estimate of anticipated expenses related to execution of the relevant bill must be submitted at the same time.[40] When a bill is proposed or submitted, the Speaker distributes it to the National Assembly members, reports it to the plenary session, and transmits it to the competent standing committee. After completion of examination by the standing committee, the Speaker refers it to the plenary session.[41] When a bill involves considerable outlays from the budget or other funds, the competent committee examining the bill must consult with the Special Committee on Budget and Accounts.[42] Any bill that a committee has determined will not be referred to the plenary session is automatically repealed, unless thirty or more members request that it be sent to the plenary session within seven days of such committee decision.[43]

---

[33] *19th National Assembly Election Results Map*, KOREA HERALD (Apr. 12, 2012), http://www.koreaherald.com/view.php?ud=20120412001212, *archived at* https://perma.cc/XTJ5-96K3.

[34] NATIONAL ASSEMBLY, *supra* note 25.

[35] *Voter Turnout Data for Korea, Republic of*, INSTITUTE FOR DEMOCRATIC AND ELECTORAL ASSISTANCE, http://www.idea.int/vt/countryview.cfm?CountryCode=KR (last updated Oct. 5, 2011), *archived at* https://perma.cc/MX66-KTRU.

[36] Yongwook Ryu, *South Korea's 2012 National Assembly Elections*, EAST ASIA FORUM (Apr. 25, 2012), http://www.eastasiaforum.org/2012/04/25/south-korea-s-2012-national-assembly-elections, *archived at* https://perma.cc/6XMN-6M7W.

[37] *Id.*

[38] CONSTITUTION art. 52.

[39] National Assembly Act art. 79(1).

[40] *Id.* art. 79-2.

[41] *Id.* art. 81(1).

[42] *Id.* art. 83-2(1).

[43] *Id.* art. 87.

A bill passed by the National Assembly is transferred by the Speaker to the President, and the President promulgates the bill within fifteen days.[44] If the President objects to the bill, he or she may return it to the National Assembly and request that it be reconsidered within the fifteen-day period.[45] The President cannot propose amendments.[46] If the National Assembly repasses the bill in the original form with the attendance of more than one-half of the total members, and with a concurrent vote of two-thirds or more of the members present, it becomes an act.[47]

A budget bill is formulated and submitted to the National Assembly by the Executive within ninety days before the beginning of each fiscal year. The National Assembly must decide upon it within thirty days before the beginning of the fiscal year.[48] If the budget bill is not passed by the beginning of the fiscal year, the Executive may, in conformity with the budget of the previous fiscal year, disburse funds for certain continuation purposes until the budget bill is passed by the National Assembly.[49]

---

[44] CONSTITUTION art. 53(1); National Assembly Act art. 98.

[45] CONSTITUTION art. 53(2).

[46] *Id.* art. 53(3).

[47] *Id.* art. 53(4).

[48] *Id.* art. 54(2).

[49] *Id.* art. 54(3).

Sweden

Elin Hofverberg
Foreign Law Research Consultant

SUMMARY Sweden is a constitutional monarchy with a parliamentary system of government and unicameral Parliament. There are twenty-nine electoral districts and elections are held every four years. Parties must receive 4% of the national vote to receive seats in the Parliament.

Legislation is initiated by the Government or individual members of Parliament and researched by parliamentary committees; it is often vetted by the Law Council before being brought for a vote. Bills are generally passed by simple majority except for changes to the Constitution or the Parliamentary Working Order (Riksdagsordning), which require two separate votes. Voting on the budget bill is controlled by special legislation. The Parliament has met in the same building since 1905.

I. Background

A. Sweden

Sweden is a kingdom that was first united in the sixteenth century by Gustav Vasa.[1] The King still serves as the formal head of state,[2] while executive powers reside in the Prime Minister and his or her government.[3] The Parliament represents the people and has the power to legislate.[4]

B. Creation of Parliament

The history of the creation of the Swedish Parliament is not straightforward. A meeting in 1435, where representatives from different parts of Sweden met in Arboga to discuss national matters, has been called the first parliamentary meeting (the Arboga meeting) but it was not until two national assemblies in Västerås in 1527 and 1544 that representatives from the four estates (nobility, clergy, bourgeoisie, and farmers) met.[5]

---

[1] *Att styra, skatta och bedöma,* STATENS FASTIGHETSVERK, http://www.sfv.se/sv/bygg-pa-kunskap/vara-byggnadsminnen-berattar-historien/arkitekturens-stilar-och-ismer (last visited Dec. 8, 2015), *archived at* https://perma.cc/D5JX-MBUL.

[2] 1 ch. 5 § REGERINGSFORMEN [RF] [CONSTITUTION].

[3] *Id.* 1 ch. 6 §.

[4] *Id.* 1 ch. 1-4 §§.

[5] *Riksdagens historia,* SVERIGES RIKSDAG (Feb. 26, 2015), http://www.riksdagen.se/sv/Sa-funkar-riksdagen/Demokrati/Riksdagens-historia, *archived at* https://perma.cc/Y5EL-56GS.

The national meetings were called *Riksdag* (Parliament) starting in the 1540s.[6] However, real parliamentary meetings were not set up until the 1600s. This was followed by two hundred years of varying parliamentary influence.[7]

C. The Parliament Building

The actual Parliament Building that houses the Swedish Parliament, located between Old Town Stockholm and the rest of the city, was erected in 1905.[8] Prior to 1905 the Parliament met at Stockholm Castle and the Old Parliament Building.[9]

D. Developments

In 1809 a new Constitution was promulgated (in force until 1974), which gave the Parliament greater powers.[10] It also set up other functions, such as the court system and a Justitieombudsman (Justice Ombudsman) to whom citizens could turn with grievances against state agencies.[11]

Women gained the right to vote in 1921, which was also the first year that women were elected to Parliament, then consisting of two chambers.[12]

Until 1971 the Swedish Parliament was bicameral, one house having indirect representation with members elected by regional governments and the other elected through direct elections.[13]

Between 1971 and 1975, the Parliament had 350 members (and votes), which turned out to be difficult as it meant that, in theory, the votes could be split equally in two.[14] Several legislative proposals put forward during the period from 1973 to 1975 resulted in a draw.[15] Therefore, the number of seats was reduced to 349 in 1976.[16]

---

[6] *Id.*

[7] *See id.*

[8] *Gamla riksdagshuset på Riddarholmen*, STATENS FASTIGHETSVERK, http://www.sfv.se/sv/fastigheter/sverige/ stockholms-lan-ab/riddarholmen/gamla-riksdagshuset-pa-riddarholmen (last visited Dec. 4, 2015), *archived at* https://perma.cc/A9KM-CG2S.

[9] *Id.*

[10] SVERIGES RIKSDAG, *supra* note 5.

[11] *Id.*

[12] *Id.*

[13] *Id.*

[14] *Id.*

[15] *Id.*

[16] *Id.*

II. Constitutional Status and Role

Sweden is a constitutional monarchy, i.e., the Monarch is the head of state but serves as a figurehead.[17] Executive power lies with the Government.[18] The role of the Parliament is to legislate, impose taxes, spend revenue, and provide oversight of the Government.[19]

Regional municipalities have a constitutionally established right of independence.[20] The municipalities are responsible for schools and health care, while the state is responsible for the police, defense, and similar national interests.[21]

III. Structure and Composition

A. General

The Parliament is unicameral with 349 seats. There are currently eight parties in the Parliament—the Social Democrats have 113 seats (31.01%), the Moderates eighty-four seats (23.33%), the Swedish Democrats forty-eight seats (12.86%), the Liberals nineteen seats (5.42%), the Center Party twenty-two seats (6.11%), the Left twenty-one seats (5.72%), the Greens twenty-five seats (6.89%), and the Christian Democrats sixteen seats (4.57%).[22] One need not be a Member of Parliament (MP) to be a chairperson of a political party. For instance, Ebba Busch Thor of the Christian Democrats is not an MP.[23] In party leadership debates in the Parliament she is represented by the leader of her party.[24]

The members represent regional constituencies, with each region represented proportionally, i.e., not by a winner-takes-all system. There are 310 seats divided by county and an additional thirty-

---

[17] 1 ch. 5 § RF.

[18] 1 ch. 6 § RF.

[19] 1 ch. 4 § RF.

[20] 1 ch. 1 § RF. *See also* KOMMUNALLAGEN (Svensk författningssamling [SFS] 1991:900), https://www.notisum.se/rnp/sls/lag/19910900 htm, *archived at* https://perma.cc/H79X-TL5M.

[21] *Försvarsdepartementet*, REGERINGSKANSLIET, http://www.regeringen.se/sveriges-regering/forsvars departementet, *archived at* https://perma.cc/F5ER-N4MS; 10 ch. 24 § SKOLLAGEN (SFS 2010:800), https://www.notisum.se/rnp/sls/lag/20100800.htm, *archived at* https://perma.cc/ZHA7-3KWP; *see also* SOU 2005:84 EN NY UPPGIFTS- OCH ANSVARSFÖRDELNING MELLAN POLIS OCH ÅKLAGARE at 133, http://www.regeringen.se/contentassets/9cf5b92d893641a4a0a3b99ed2687d93/en-ny-uppgifts--och-ansvarsfordelning-mellan-polis-och-aklagare-del-2, *archived at* https://perma.cc/D84W-KD9W.

[22] *Val till riksdagen – Röster*, VALMYNDIGHETEN (Sept. 19, 2014), http://www.val.se/val/val2014/slutresultat/R/rike/index html, *archived at* https://perma.cc/VHS9-WG38.

[23] *Ebba Busch Thor*, RIKSDAGEN, http://www riksdagen.se/sv/ledamoter-partier/Ej-invalda-personer/Ebba-Busch-Thor (last visited Dec. 4, 2015), *archived at* https://perma.cc/T9YT-AC4F.

[24] Emelie Nyman, *Doldisen ska axla Busch Thors mantel*, SVD (Oct. 13, 2015), http://www.svd.se/doldisen-ska-axla-ebba-busch-thors-mantel, *archived at* https://perma.cc/Q9WV-VLT6.

nine seats that are "adjustment" seats, meaning seats filled to better reflect the election results.[25] The numbers of permanent seats versus adjustment seats are established by the Central Elections Authority no later than April 30 of the year in which the national election takes place.[26]

The counties are listed in law.[27] The counties and the number of seats are as follows: Skåne County South, thirteen seats; Skåne County West, eleven seats; City of Malmö, eleven seats; Skåne County North and East, thirteen seats; Halland County, twelve seats; Blekinge County, five seats; Kronoberg County, six seats; Kalmar County, eight seats; Jönköping Country, thirteen seats; Västra Gotaland County South, six seats; City of Gothenburg, seventeen seats; Västra Götaland County West, thirteen seats; Västra Götaland County North, thirteen seats; Västra Götaland County East, ten seats; Östergötland County, fifteen seats; Södermanland County, eleven seats; Stockholm County, thirty-nine seats; Värmland County, eleven seats; Örebro County, twelve seats; Västmanland County, ten seats; Uppsala County, twelve seats; Gävleborg County, eleven seats; Dalarna County, eleven seats; Jämtland County, four seats; Västernorrland County, ten seats; Västerbotten County, ten seats; Norrbotten County, eight seats; and Gotland County, two seats.[28]

The distribution of seats is regulated in chapter 14 of the Election Law.[29] Seats are calculated by the following formula:

> 3 § The permanent mandates shall for each electoral district be distributed proportionally between parties that are part of the distribution. The distribution takes place by the use of a "comparable value" which is calculated for the parties based on the election results in the that electorate. The party that at each calculation gets the largest comparative value is awarded a mandate/seat.
>
> . . . The calculation shall be done by using an adjusted odd-number method. This means that as long as one party has not received a seat the comparative value is calculated by the party's votes in the electoral divided by 1,2. When the party has gotten a mandate a new comparative value is calculated by the party's votes divided by 3. Thereafter the process continues by dividing the party's votes with the closest highest odd-number for each awarded seat. Lag (2014:1384).[30]

---

[25] *Så fördelas platserna i riksdagen*, SVERIGES RIKSDAG (June 24, 2014), http://www.riksdagen.se/sv/Sa-funkar-riksdagen/Demokrati/Val-till-riksdagen/Sa-fordelas-platserna-i-riksdagen, *archived at* https://perma.cc/XF52-4NVH.

[26] 4 ch. 3 § VALLAG (SFS 2005:837), https://www.notisum.se/rnp/sls/lag/20050837.htm, *archived at* https://perma.cc/Q38A-CF4Y.

[27] *Id.* 4 ch. 2 §.

[28] *Members and Parties*, RIKSDAGEN, http://www.riksdagen.se/en/Members-and-parties (last visited Nov. 4, 2015), *archived at* http://perma.cc/P8EM-F9Q3.

[29] 14 ch. VALLAGEN.

[30] *Id.* 3 §.

4 § To determine how many seats a party should have in total in the Parliament in order to be proportionally represented in the entire country, [the same] adjusted odd-number method is applied using the entire country as an electoral district. Lag (2014:1384).[31]

The establishment of electoral regions is based on the national census registry as it exists on the first of March of the election year.[32]

Parties must receive a threshold of 4% of the vote nationally or 12% in an election precinct to receive a seat in Parliament. In certain areas, such as Gotland, which only has two seats, 12% is not sufficient to receive a seat.

B. Committees

There are fifteen committees in parliament, two of which are prescribed in the Constitution (the Committee on the Constitution and the Committee on Finance):[33]

- Committee on Civil Affairs
- Committee on the Constitution
- Committee on Cultural Affairs
- Committee on Defense
- Committee on Education
- Committee on Environment and Agriculture
- Committee on Finance
- Committee on Foreign Affairs
- Committee on Health and Welfare
- Committee on Industry and Trade
- Committee on Justice
- Committee on the Labor Market
- Committee on Social Insurance
- Committee on Taxation
- Committee on Transport and Communications[34]

---

[31] *Id.* 3–4 §§.

[32] *Id* 4 §.

[33] 4 ch. 3 § RF.

[34] 7 ch. 2 § Addendum 7.2.1 to RIKSDAGSORDNINGEN (SFS 2014:801), https://www.notisum.se/rnp/sls/lag/20140801.htm, *archived at* https://perma.cc/QG83-54GZ; *see also The 15 Parliamentary Committees*, SVERIGES RIKSDAG (Oct. 1, 2015), http://www.riksdagen.se/en/Committees/The-15-parliamentary-committees, *archived at* https://perma.cc/M2S4-WZBF.

There is also a Committee on European Union Affairs.[35]

The Parliament may constitute additional committees, and if it does it must provide a description of the work to be done in the committee.[36] Each committee must have an uneven number of members and not less than fifteen members.[37] The committees must work together with the Committee on EU Affairs when the work so requires.[38]

The role of a committee is to consider legislation in the committee's subject area, such as defense.[39]

Work in the committees take place behind closed doors.[40] Meetings may, however, take place in public if the committee considers it necessary in order to obtain information related to its legislative work.[41] The purpose of such public committee meetings is to hold committee hearings.[42]

C. Law Council

Before a bill is presented to Parliament the proposed legislation must be reviewed by the Law Council if the legislation pertains to certain issues, including constitutional changes to press freedoms, access to public documents, treatment of personal data, and municipal obligations.[43] The Law Council reviews legislation to determine how the proposal holds up against the Constitution and law and order generally, how the provisions of the text relate to each other and relate to the rule of law, whether the legislation furthers its stated purpose, and whether there are any problems that might occur during application of the law.[44] The composition of the Law Council is regulated by law.[45]

The Law Council's reports are published on its website.[46]

---

[35] *The Committee on European Union Affairs*, SVERIGES RIKSDAG (Oct. 7, 2014), http://www riksdagen. se/en/Committees/The-Committee-on-European-Union-Affairs, *archived at* https://perma.cc/K53V-5VGG.

[36] Tilläggsbestämmelse 7.2.2 [Addendum 7.2.2.] Riksdagsordningen.

[37] 7 ch. 4 § Riksdagsordningen.

[38] *Id.* 7 ch. 15 §.

[39] *Id.* 7 ch. 5, 8–10 §§.

[40] *Id.* 7 ch. 16 §.

[41] *Id.* 7 ch. 17 §.

[42] *See* Jenny Jonasson & Ingvar Åkesson, Comment 157, *in* KARNOV SVENSK LAGSAMLING MED KOMMENTARER 2014/2015 at 45 (comment to the previous Riksdagsordning SFS 1974:153).

[43] 8 ch. 21 § RF.

[44] *Id.* 8 ch. 22 §.

[45] LAG OM LAGRÅDET [ACT ON THE LAW COUNCIL] (SFS 2003:333), http://www notisum.se/rnp/sls/lag/ 20030333.htm, *archived at* https://perma.cc/NK3M-A7PD.

[46] LAGRÅDET, http://www.lagradet.se (last visited Dec. 8, 2015), *archived at* https://perma.cc/T2WL-FYMB.

D. Speaker of the Parliament

There is one Speaker of the Parliament (*talmannen*)[47] and three deputies.[48] By tradition the Speaker of the House is a representative from the largest party, the First Vice Speaker is a representative of the second largest party, the Second Vice Speaker is a representative of the third largest party, and the Third Vice Speaker is a representative of the fourth largest party. Following the 2014 election there was great debate surrounding the Speaker, as the third largest party was the Sweden Democrats.[49] Prior to this election, the remaining seven parties in Parliament had made a point of not working with the party and several MPs were very concerned that this anti-immigration party would represent Sweden. In the end the Sweden Democrats did receive the second deputy position.[50]

The Speaker of the House can act as temporary head of state.[51] The Speaker suggests when a vote on a particular bill must be held.[52] The Speaker also initiates the selection of the Prime Minister (see Part IV, below).

IV. Elections

A. General Election Cycle

The Parliament meets annually.[53] Elections occur four years apart,[54] on the second Sunday in September.[55] The next election will be on September 9, 2018. Results of the 2014 election are published on the Election Agency's website.[56] Prior to 1994 the election cycle was three years.[57]

There are no term limits for individual members of Parliament, their leaders, or the Prime Minister. The longest ruling party is the Social Democrats who have been in government

---

[47] *The Speaker*, SVERIGES RIKSDAG, http://www.riksdagen.se/en/How-the-Riksdag-works/The-Speaker, *archived at* https://perma.cc/4G4Z-VTHB.

[48] 4 ch. 2 § RF.

[49] *Obefintligh chans att SD får talmanspost*, SVD (Sept. 18, 2015), http://www.svd.se/obefintlig-chans-att-sd-far-talmanspost, *archived at* https://perma.cc/YCK2-EX8A.

[50] *SD får vice talmanspost*, SVT (Sept. 18, 2014), http://www.svt.se/nyheter/val2014/sd-far-vice-talmanspost, *archived at* https://perma.cc/YJY2-GJ92; *Vice talmän*, SVERIGES RIKSDAG (Dec. 15, 2014), http://www.riksdagen.se/sv/Sa-funkar-riksdagen/Talmannen/Vice-talman, *archived at* https://perma.cc/TGK7-2FL9.

[51] 5 ch. 7 § 2 para. RF.

[52] 9 ch. 3 § RIKSDAGSORDNINGEN.

[53] 4 ch. 1 § RF.

[54] *Id.* 3 ch. 3 §.

[55] 1 ch. 3 § 1 para. VALLAGEN (SFS 2005:837), https://www.riksdagen.se/sv/Dokument-Lagar/Lagar/Svenskforfattningssamling/sfs_sfs-2005-837, *archived at* https://perma.cc/2RJU-WRYP.

[56] *Val till riksdagen – Röster*, *supra* note 22.

[57] SVERIGES RIKSDAG, *supra* note 5.

(coalition or simple majority) for forty-four continuous years from 1932 to 1976, and for seventy of the last one hundred years.[58]

Elections are direct and secret.[59] Voters may cast a vote for a party or for an individual of a party (so called *personröst*).[60] Every citizen eighteen years and older who resides or has resided in Sweden is eligible to vote or to be elected in the parliamentary election.[61]

B. Extraordinary Elections

The Government (Regeringen) can announce extraordinary elections under special circumstances.[62] An extraordinary election has been held only once in Sweden's history, in 1958.[63] In 2014 the current Prime Minister Stefan Löfven of the Social Democrats stated that he would announce an extraordinary election but later cancelled it.[64]

C. Electoral Voting System

A representative electoral system is in place for parliamentary seats. As stated above, there are twenty-nine electoral districts in Sweden. Of the 349 seats in Parliament, 310 are "firm" representatives while an additional thirty-nine seats are adjustments seats, distributed between the parties to better reflect the national voter outcome.[65] A party must receive at least 4% of the national vote to receive seats in Parliament.[66]

Voter participation in parliamentary elections is generally high. In 2014, voter turnout was 85.81%, up from 84.63% in 2010.[67]

D. Formation of Parliament/Government

Following a general election, the formation of Parliament is initiated by the Speaker of the House, who, after discussions with party leadership and the vice speakers, announces who he or

---

[58] *Swedish Social Democratic Party (SAP)*, ENCYCLOPÆDIA BRITANNICA, http://www.britannica.com/topic/ Swedish-Social-Democratic-Party, (last visited Dec. 8, 2015), *archived at* https://perma.cc/AP6H-A927.

[59] 3 ch. 1 § RF.

[60] *Id.*

[61] *Id.* 3 ch. 4 §.

[62] *Id.* 3 ch. 11 §.

[63] *Extra val*, SVERIGES RIKSDAG (Dec. 22, 2014), http://www.riksdagen.se/sv/Sa-funkar-riksdagen/Demokrati/Val-till-riksdagen/Extra-val, *archived at* https://perma.cc/4HBT-2Y9M.

[64] Tomas Ramberg, *Tomas Ramberg: Extravalet som inte blev av*, SVERIGES RADIO (Mar. 22, 2015), http://sverigesradio.se/sida/artikel.aspx?programid=83&artikel=6122886, *archived at* https://perma.cc/L2KN-L4BK.

[65] 3 ch. 6 § RF.

[66] *Id.* 3 ch. 7 §.

[67] *Val till Riksdagen – Röster, supra* note 22.

she proposes as responsible for constituting a government.[68] The Parliament then votes for or against the suggested Prime Minister, and provided the majority is not against the Prime Minister he or she is allowed to form a government.[69] This rule was adopted in 2010 to allow for minority governments to form more easily.[70]

V. Legislative Process

A. Budget Bill

The adoption of a budget bill follows special rules.[71] A budget bill should be presented no later than September 20 of each year.[72] In an election year (elections are held in September, see Part IV(A), above) the budget proposal should be presented to Parliament no later than two weeks after the parliamentary session has started.[73]

By tradition, parties have either voted for their own bill or abstained from voting. In 2014 the Swedish Democrats voted for the Alliance (opposition) budget, which thus received more votes than the Government (Social Democrat and Green Party) budget. The move was a first in Swedish politics. As a result, the Alliance budget bill passed and the Government had to use the opposition budget to govern the country. Changes were made in the spring adjustment budget, but not until fall 2015 could the Government present its own budget.

As a result, with the intention of ensuring that the Government would be able to pass its budgets, six parties (the Social Democrats, the Green Party, the Moderates, the Center Party, the Liberals, and the Christian Democrats) agreed to not vote against the ruling Government's bill between 2015 and 2022.[74] The agreement was called the Decemberöverenskommelsen (DÖ),[75] and received considerable criticism for not being democratic, as the opposition effectively could not vote for its own proposals in fear that the Swedish Democrats would vote for them as well.[76] The agreement was voted down by the General Meeting of the Christian Democrat Party on

---

[68] 6 ch. 4 § RF.

[69] Id.

[70] Id. See Prop. 2009/2010:80 En reformerad grundlag at 108, http://www.regeringen.se/contentassets/095135 b9032c46afacf5e0a8a55389e1/en-reformerad-grundlag-prop.-20091080, archived at https://perma.cc/6F9G-RP84.

[71] BUDGETLAG (SFS 2011:203), https://www.notisum.se/rnp/sls/lag/20110203.htm, archived at https://perma.cc/8T8X-V2FK.

[72] TILLÄGGSBESTÄMMELSE 9.5.1[ADDENDUM 9.5.1 TO] RIKSDAGSORDNINGEN.

[73] Id.

[74] Överrenskommelsen, KRISTDEMOKRATERNA, https://kristdemokraterna.se/Global/pdf/December%c3%b6veren skommelsen.pdf (last visited Dec. 4, 2015), archived at https://perma.cc/6YV2-2MT8.

[75] Id.

[76] Så fungerar decemberöverenskommelsen, DAGENSNYHETER (Dec. 27, 2015), http://www.dn.se/nyheter/politik/sa-fungerar-decemberoverenskommelsen, archived at http://perma.cc/64LN-VCX8.

October 9, 2015.[77] On the same day the Moderate party announced that by the Christian Democrats' leaving the agreement the agreement had in fact been broken and no longer bound the other five parties.[78] The Alliance did not present a common budget in the fall of 2015.

B. All Other Bills

New legislation is initiated through proposals (*motioner*) presented by individual MPs or groups of MPs, which are then researched and recommended for votes by committees, then voted on by Parliament. Government proposals are also voted on by Parliament.[79] A simple majority is enough for all bills except the budget bill (see above) and proposals to change the Constitution.

Special voting is required for the four pieces of legislation that make up the Constitution (Riksdagsförordningen, Tryckfrihetsförordningen, Yttrandefrihetsgrundlagen, and Successionsordningen) as well as for the Riksdagsordning (not part of the Constitution but a special law that regulates how Parliament operates). Amendments to these acts require a majority in two separate voting sessions, with a general election in between.[80] In addition, the Parliamentary Working Order may also be amended by one single vote provided that at least three-fourths of the voting MPs constituting at least half of all MPs approve the bill.[81]

---

[77] Ebba Busch Thor, *Kristdemokraterna lämnar Decemberöverenskommelsen*, KRISTDEMOKRATERNA (Oct. 9, 2015), https://kristdemokraterna.se/Media/Nyhetsarkiv/Kristdemokraterna-sager-xx-till-Decemberoverenskommelsen, *archived at* https://perma.cc/7S2C-QJUW.

[78] Viktor Mölne, *Kinberg Batra: Jag kan konstatera att överenskommelsen är upphävd*, DAGENS INDUSTRI (Oct. 9, 2015), http://www.di.se/artiklar/2015/10/9/kinberg-batra-jag-kan-konstatera-att-overenskommelsen-ar-upphavd, *archived at* http://perma.cc/XD29-JSEL (click "Screen capture" tab).

[79] 9 ch. 2 § RIKSDAGSORDNINGEN.

[80] 8 ch. 14 § RF.

[81] *Id.* 8 ch. 17 §.

United Kingdom

Clare Feikert-Ahalt
Senior Foreign Law Specialist

SUMMARY   The United Kingdom's Parliament took centuries to develop into the institution that it is today, and its role continues to evolve. Created initially as a way to allow the Crown to collect taxes from his or her subjects, the powers of Parliament gradually expanded to supplement and then act on behalf of the Crown in almost all areas. Parliament has met at Westminster, in London, for centuries.

The electoral process is heavily regulated by legislation and the "first past the post" system was recently affirmed by a national referendum. The frequency that Parliament must call elections was recently affirmed in statute as being every five years.

I. Background

The United Kingdom of Great Britain and Northern Ireland (UK) is the collective name of four countries—England, Wales, Scotland, and Northern Ireland. The four separate countries were united under a single Parliament in London, known as the Parliament at Westminster, through a series of Acts of Union.[1] The UK has undergone a period of devolution over the past twenty years with the creation of a Scottish Parliament, a National Assembly in Wales, and an Assembly in Northern Ireland.

The UK does not have a formal written constitution; thus, there is no provision that specifically allocates responsibilities and powers to the legislative or executive branches. Instead, the distribution of responsibilities is governed by long-established custom and conventions. It is customary law that the Crown, as the head of state, acts on the advice of the relevant Ministers.[2]

A. Establishment Of The Legislature

The year 2015 marked the 750th anniversary of the Parliament that was summoned by the baronial leader Simon De Montfort in 1265.[3] While this was not the first Parliament seen in

---

[1] Stat Wallie 1284, 12 Edw. 1 (*repealed*); Union with Scotland Act 1706, 6 Ann c. 11, *as amended*; Union with Ireland Act 1800, 38 & 40 Geo. 3 c. 67; Government of Ireland Act 1920, 10 & 11 Geo. 5 c. 67 (*repealed*), http://www.legislation.gov.uk/ukpga/1920/67/pdfs/ukpga_19200067_en.pdf, *archived at* https://perma.cc/F2S6-ZX5S.

[2] "There is a well-established rule that the making of a treaty is an Executive act, while the performance of its obligations, if they entail alteration of the existing domestic law, requires legislative action." Att'y Gen. for Canada v. Att'y Gen. for Ontario [1937] A.C. 326 [347] (H.L.).

[3] HISTORY OF PARLIAMENT TRUST, THE STORY OF PARLIAMENT, foreword (2015).

England, as "there is no date that marks the exact beginning of parliament,"[4] this Parliament is seen as the prototype for Parliament as we know it today,[5] in that it included representatives from counties and towns across England, demonstrating to the King that he could no longer make decisions for the entire country without input from a wide group of people.[6]

B. General History and Development

The Magna Carta of 1215 limited the methods by which the King could collect monies, and this limitation on money-collection methods was reaffirmed by the Magna Cartas issued in 1216 and 1217. This limitation forced the King to turn to taxation, which required the consent of his subjects. In 1265, King Henry III was held captive and a revolutionary regime headed by Simon de Montford confirmed the Magna Carta in a Parliament comprised of elected knights and townsmen.[7] The Magna Carta was confirmed again by Edward I, Henry II's son, in the Parliaments of 1297 and 1300.[8]

The centuries that followed involved power struggles between the Crown (the King—see Part II, below) and Parliament. In the year 1376, the Parliament known as "The Good Parliament" showed for the first time that it had the potential to limit the powers of the Crown by prosecuting royal officials through a newly created procedure of impeachment.[9]

The sixteenth century saw the Reformation, where King Henry VIII rejected the Catholic Church and established a national, royal church, later to become known as the Church of England, which served to enhance the standing of Parliament.[10] Parliament was still summoned primarily to provide the King with the ability to tax his subjects, the revenues from which were commonly used to conduct wars.[11]

By the early seventeenth century, Parliament had become a prominent part of the political landscape, which led to confrontations between the King and leading Members of Parliament[12] and the outbreak of two civil wars, the latter resulting in the beheading of King Charles I on January 3, 1649.[13] The period 1649–60 was known as the Interregnum, when England was ruled as a Republican nation. Power was vested mainly in the "Rump Parliament," which abolished both the House of Lords

---

[4] *Id.* at 8. Page 12 of this book notes that the first Parliament could be dated to the reign of King Athelstan (924–39), but this "Parliament" was a royal assembly of nobles and churchmen rather than a parliament as would be recognized today.

[5] *Id,.* foreword.

[6] *Id.* at 9.

[7] *Id.* at 15.

[8] *Id.*

[9] *Id.* at 20.

[10] *Id.* at 34.

[11] *Id.* at 38.

[12] *Id.* at 35.

[13] *Id.* at 35.

and the Monarchy. In 1653, Oliver Cromwell forcibly dissolved the Rump Parliament, and army commanders appointed 140 members to a new assembly, known as the "Barebones Parliament." This Parliament appointed Cromwell as Lord Protector of England, Scotland, and Ireland. The Protectorate Parliament succeeded the Barebones Parliament; however, it was not a success and paved the way to military rule, which was extremely unpopular. The Rump Parliament was later reinstated and, voted that the government should be led by a king, returned Charles II, the son of Charles I, to the throne.[14] The return from republican state to monarchy became known as the Restoration. Charles II called few Parliaments and was succeeded by James II. James II was unpopular and was eventually overthrown by Prince William of Orange, the leader of the Dutch Republic. With William's consent, a new Parliament was called in 1689 and offered the Crown to William and his wife, Mary.[15]

The Act of Union of 1707[16] united the country of Scotland with England and Wales to form the country of Great Britain. This Act was followed almost one hundred years later by the Act of Union 1801, which united the entire country of Ireland with Great Britain.[17] Later, the majority of Ireland would become an independent country,[18] leaving a small section of the north, known as Northern Ireland, as part of Great Britain, to form the United Kingdom of Great Britain and Northern Ireland.

The government continued to evolve over the next three centuries, and its powers steadily expanded while the powers of the Crown were diminished, to the extent that, today, the role of the Monarch is largely ceremonial.

C. Moving Parliament

The British Houses of Parliament are located at the Palace of Westminster. Members of the House of Lords and the House of Commons sit in separate chambers within the building. Parliament is assembled by a writ of summons from the Crown that names the day and place of the meeting, which has traditionally been at the Palace of Westminster.[19]

There are no specific laws that grant or deny Parliament the authority to continue its responsibilities if it cannot meet due to some event or emergency situation, although decisions can be taken only with a quorum of forty.[20] Despite this restriction, the number of House

---

[14] *Id.* at 63.

[15] *Id.* at 73.

[16] Stat Wallie 1284, 12 Edw. 1 (*repealed*); Union with Scotland Act 1706, 6 Ann c. 11, *as amended*.

[17] Union with Ireland Act 1800, 38 & 40 Geo. 3, c. 67.

[18] Government of Ireland Act 1920, 10 & 11 Geo. 5 c. 67 (*repealed*), http://www.legislation.gov.uk/ukpga/1920/67/pdfs/ukpga_19200067_en.pdf, *archived at* https://perma.cc/F2S6-ZX5S.

[19] ERSKINE MAY'S TREATISE ON THE LAW, PRIVILEGES, PROCEEDINGS AND USAGE OF PARLIAMENT 59 (C.J. Boulton et al., eds., 24th ed. 2011).

[20] House of Commons Standing Order No. 41 states as follows:

> 41.–(1)If it should appear that fewer than forty Members (including the occupant of the chair and the tellers) have taken part in a division, the business under consideration shall stand over until the next sitting of the House and the next business shall be taken.

Members present cannot formally be counted;[21] however, there are a number of ways a quorum can be ascertained, notably through a division.[22] If a quorum is not met, the business before the House stands over to another sitting, and the House proceeds to the next item of business.[23]

There was a confidential plan for the evacuation of Parliament to a secret location (later revealed as Stratford-upon-Avon) prior to the commencement of World War II, although this plan was never used.[24] During the war, Parliament was forced to convene outside of its traditional setting after the chambers of the House of Commons were destroyed during an air raid. Until it was rebuilt in 1950, the House of Commons sat at Church Road House, which was made an annex of Westminster. This adjustment resulted in the meeting place of the House remaining technically unchanged.[25] The House of Lords made its chambers available for use by the House of Commons and moved its sittings to the King's Robing Room. For the remainder of the war years there was a ban on disclosing the location of Parliament.[26]

II. Constitutional Status and Role

The UK is a constitutional monarchy. The Crown is the Head of State and has legal powers, although these are now largely ceremonial. The Crown must act upon the advice of its Ministers, who form the executive and are appointed by the Prime Minister. Ministers are typically elected Members of Parliament and thus are required to answer for their actions in Parliament.[27] The term "Crown" often refers interchangeably to either the Monarch or executive, although as the powers of the Monarch have been drastically reduced, the term is used primarily to refer to the executive branch of the government, which is deemed to act on the Monarch's behalf.

III. Structure and Composition

The UK has a bicameral Parliament consisting of the House of Lords (the Upper House composed of both hereditary and life peers[28]) and the House of Commons (the elected Lower House). The legislature debates issues and votes upon bills. A bill is generally first debated in

---

(2)The House shall not be counted at any time.

The text is available at http://www.publications.parliament.uk/pa/cm201213/cmstords/614/body.htm#BABEJHIHA, *archived at* https://perma.cc/CZP8-CMG9.

[21] *Id.* 41(2).

[22] A division is the way the House "ascertains the number of Members for and against a proposition when the Chair's opinion as to which side is in the majority on a Question is challenged." PAUL EVANS, HANDBOOK OF HOUSE OF COMMONS PROCEDURE 196 (1st ed. 1997).

[23] House of Commons Standing Order No. 41(1).

[24] JENNIFER TANFIELD, HOUSE OF COMMONS LIBRARY, IN PARLIAMENT 1939–50: THE EFFECT OF THE WAR ON THE PALACE OF WESTMINSTER, 1991, House of Commons Library Document No. 20, at 5.

[25] *Id.*

[26] *Id.*

[27] SIR WILLIAM WADE, ADMINISTRATIVE LAW (8th ed. 2000).

[28] *See* House of Lords Act 1999, c. 34, http://www.legislation.gov.uk/ukpga/1999/34, *archived at* https://perma.cc/485K-VQLR. This Act provided for the gradual abolishment of hereditary peers.

the House of Commons and, if passed by a majority vote, continues to the House of Lords, which debates it and recommends changes or amendments. The bill then passes back to the House of Commons, which considers any amendments. If both Houses agree, the bill receives Royal Assent and becomes law.

There are currently 650 Members of the House of Commons and 790 Members of the House of Lords who are eligible to sit.[29] The number of Members of the House of Commons has varied, and section 11 of the Parliamentary Voting System and Constituencies Act 2011 reduces the number of Members to six hundred, although this provision has yet to come into effect.[30]

The major parties within the UK, in order of seats won in the 2015 election, are the Conservative party, the Labour Party, the Scottish National Party, the Liberal Democrats, the UK Independence Party, the Green Party, the Democratic Unionist Party, Plaid Cymru (the Party of Wales), Sinn Fein, the Ulster Unionist Party, and the Independent Party.[31] There are a number of smaller parties, such as the Monster Raving Looney Party, but these are niche parties that are often not represented in Parliament.

As there are 650 seats in Parliament, 326 seats are needed to obtain a majority of the House. The party that gets the majority of votes goes on to form the government.

A. Committees

There are numerous parliamentary committees that discuss the reform or creation of new laws and policies and are pivotal to the development of new legislation. The committees generally consist of between ten to fifty Members of Parliament who examine government expenditure, policy, and laws in detail, and make recommendations and proposals regarding steps that should be taken to correct any issues.[32] There are Joint Committees, which consist of Members of both Houses—the Commons and the Lords. General Committees work within the Commons and consider proposed legislation. These General Committees include those that used to be known as Standing Committees. There are three Grand Committees that consider questions on Scotland, Wales and Northern Ireland.[33]

---

[29] *Who's in the House of Lords*, PARLIAMENT.UK, http://www.parliament.uk/business/lords/whos-in-the-house-of-lords (last visited Dec. 23, 2015), *archived at* https://perma.cc/9UKY-S2P8.

[30] Parliamentary Voting System and Constituencies Act 2011 c. 1, § 11, http://www.legislation.gov.uk/ukpga/2011/1/enacted, *archived at* http://perma.cc/XH5U-35EJ.

[31] *Political Parties in Parliament*, PARLIAMENT.UK, http://www.parliament.uk/about/mps-and-lords/members/parties (last visited Dec. 28, 2015), *archived at* https://perma.cc/K7EG-FDDX.

[32] ROBERT ROGERS AND RHODRI WALTERS, HOW PARLIAMENT WORKS 306 (7th ed. 2015).

[33] *Committees*, PARLIAMENT.UK, http://www.parliament.uk/about/how/committees (last visited Dec. 28, 2015), *archived at* https://perma.cc/74KG-2VHV.

B. Leadership and Whips in the House of Commons

The House of Commons is led by the Speaker of the House, who is responsible for chairing and leading debates, and keeping order in the Commons. This is the highest role within the House of Commons, and the Speaker of the House must remain impartial.[34]

Parliamentary Whips serve a number of important roles in Parliament. They work to get the government's business through Parliament, by securing majority votes on the government's legislative policy and programs.[35] The Chief Whip also has an advisory role, informing the Cabinet about the "acceptability of its legislative proposals to the parliamentary party."[36] The Chief Whip must also work to set out the schedule for the government's program of business[37] and is directly responsible to both the Prime Minister and the Leader of the House. The Chief Whip must also liaise with Ministers regarding parliamentary business that affects their departments.[38]

IV. Elections

Parliamentary elections were first introduced in medieval England as a solution from the Crown, who was required to obtain consent from Parliament to directly tax his subjects.[39] These elections evolved over time to have a detailed set of rules and procedures that continue to be refined today.

National elections are known as General Parliamentary Elections.[40] The Fixed Term Parliaments Act 2011 established five-year fixed-term Parliaments, with the election occurring on the first Thursday of May, five years after the last election was held.[41] The political party that wins the most seats during this election goes on to form the government.

A principle of the British system of government is that the government of the day must have the confidence of the House of Commons. As noted above, the government is formed by the party that wins the majority of seats during the general election. A "hung Parliament" results when no party wins a majority during the election. A report from the House of Commons states that

---

[34] *Office and Role of a Speaker*, PARLIAMENT.UK, http://www.parliament.uk/business/commons/the-speaker/the-role-of-the-speaker/role-of-the-speaker (last visited Dec. 28, 2015), *archived at* https://perma.cc/4R33-NND4.

[35] JENNIFER WALPOLE & RICHARD KELLY, HOUSE OF COMMONS LIBRARY, PARLIAMENT AND CONSTITUTION CENTRE, THE WHIP'S OFFICE, Oct. 10, 2008, Standard Note SN/PC/02829, at 4, http://researchbriefings files. parliament.uk/documents/SN02829/SN02829.pdf, *archived at* https://perma.cc/7RGV-E6VM.

[36] *Id.* at 5.

[37] ERSKINE MAY, *supra* note 19, at 51.

[38] *Id.*

[39] HISTORY OF PARLIAMENT TRUST, *supra* note 3, at 22.

[40] "Parliamentary Election" is defined as "the election of a Member to serve in Parliament for a constituency." Interpretation Act 1978, c. 30, § 5, sched. 1, http://www.legislation.gov.uk/ukpga/1978/30, *archived at* https://perma.cc/BC4D-EK57.

[41] Fixed Term Parliaments Act 2011, c. 14, § 1, http://www.legislation.gov.uk/ukpga/2011/14/contents/enacted, *archived at* http://perma.cc/2ERZ-8KFS.

"there are four likely outcomes. These [are] . . . (a) a minority government; (b) a coalition; (c) a failure to produce a government at all; or (d) two or more of these things during the lifetime of a parliament."[42]   A hung Parliament occurred during the 2010 election, and the Conservative Party and Liberal Democrats went on to form a coalition government.[43]

Prior to the Fixed Term Parliaments Act 2011, the maximum duration of a Parliament was five years, at which point Parliament automatically expired.[44] This rarely happened, however, and elections would generally occur after Parliament was dissolved, either through Royal Proclamation[45] or upon the advice of the Prime Minister.[46] The effect of the Proclamation was to vacate all the seats in the House of Commons and require a general election for the Commons. Because there was no set timetable for when an election should be held, other than it should occur within the five-year maximum term of Parliament, the Prime Minister had a political and tactical advantage of deciding the date of the general election, although generally the election was announced in the spring in which the Parliament was due to expire.

The last general election was held on May 7, 2015, and the Conservative party won 330 seats, accounting for 36.9% of votes. This secured a majority in the House for the Conservatives by twelve seats, the first time this party has secured a majority government since 1992. The next election will occur in accordance with the requirements established by the Fixed Term Parliaments Act 2011, and will take place the first Thursday in May 2020.[47]

A. Electoral System

In the UK, the electoral system used is that of a simple majority (plurality) for each constituency, more commonly known as the "first past the post" system. The candidate who wins the largest number of votes from his or her constituency is to Parliament. The political party that wins the most votes goes on to form the government. A referendum was held in 2011 in which voters were asked if they wished to change the electoral system from the first past the post system to an

---

[42] LUCINDA MAER, HOUSE OF COMMONS LIBRARY, PARLIAMENT AND CONSTITUTION CENTER, HUNG PARLIAMENTS, Mar. 17, 2010, Standard Note SN/PC/04951, http://dotat.at/tmp/hung.pdf, *archived at* https://perma.cc/4SBB-YYGU (citing Lord Norton, *The Perils of a Hung Parliament, in* NO OVERALL CONTROL? THE IMPACT OF A "HUNG PARLIAMENT" ON BRITISH POLITICS (Hansard Society 2008), http://www.hansardsociety.org.uk/wp-content/uploads/2012/10/No-Overall-Control-2008.pdf, *archived at* https://perma.cc/GGJ2-P3CX). For an updated and expanded version of this Standard Note (which does not contain Lord Norton's quote), see Lucinda Maer, House of Commons Library, Hung Parliaments in the Twentieth Century, May 8, 2015, Briefing Paper No. 04951, http://research briefings.parliament.uk/ResearchBriefing/Summary/SN04951#fullreport, *archived at* https://perma.cc/9QJC-6NUK.

[43] *Election 2010: First Hung Parliament in UK for Decades*, BBC NEWS (May 7, 2010), http://news.bbc.co.uk/2/hi/8667071.stm, *archived at* https://perma.cc/9C64-DS6T.

[44] Septennial Act 1715, c. 38, 1 Geo. 1. St. 2, *repealed by* Fixed Term Parliaments Act 2011, c. 14, § 1, http://www.legislation.gov.uk/ukpga/2011/14/contents/enacted, *archived at* http://perma.cc/2ERZ-8KFS.

[45] Representation of the People Act 1983, c. 2, sched. 1, http://www.legislation.gov.uk/ukpga/1983/2, *archived at* https://perma.cc/7T5X-2ZTU.

[46] The average term of Parliament since 1945 has been three years and seven months. ROBERT ROGERS & RHODRI WALTERS, HOW PARLIAMENT WORKS 22 (5th ed. 2004).

[47] Fixed Term Parliaments Act 2011, c. 14, § 3.

alternative voting system. Voter turnout was higher than expected at 41%, with an overwhelming majority of 67.9% of voters rejecting a change in the electoral system.[48]

Eligibility to vote in general elections in the UK is subject to a number of criteria. Primarily, the individual wishing to vote must be registered in the register of parliamentary electors for his or her relevant constituency.[49] To be able to register his or her name in the register of parliamentary electors, the individual must be a British subject, which includes Commonwealth citizens,[50] or a citizen of the Republic of Ireland residing in Britain,[51] and be eighteen years or older. A British citizen residing overseas can vote for up to fifteen years after he or she leaves the country.[52]

Individuals who are disqualified from voting are Members of the House of Lords, legal or illegal immigrants, individuals of unsound mind, individuals guilty of corrupt or illegal practices in elections, and prisoners detained while serving their sentence. This latter restriction is currently under review as a result of a successful challenge before the European Court of Justice, although the current government has stated it has no plans to provide prisoners with a vote.[53]

B. Electoral Districts

Electoral Districts in the UK are known as parliamentary constituencies, with each constituency electing one Member of Parliament. There are currently 650 constituencies in the UK, with the average population represented by a Member of Parliament being 68,000.[54] The breakdown of Members of Parliament representing the countries of the UK is as follows: 533 in England, 59 in Scotland, 40 in Wales, and 18 in Northern Ireland.[55] The distribution of these seats is under continuous review by four nondepartmental government bodies, known as the Boundary

---

[48] *Vote 2011: UK Rejects Alternative Vote*, BBC NEWS (May 7, 2011), http://www.bbc.com/news/uk-politics-13297573, *archived at* https://perma.cc/CD52-JNA5.

[49] ERSKINE MAY, *supra* note 19, at 40.

[50] Representation of the People Act 1983, c. 2, § 4(6), http://www.legislation.gov.uk/ukpga/1983/2, *archived at* https://perma.cc/KUW9-PCZX. Commonwealth citizens are individuals who do not require leave to enter or remain in the United Kingdom. *See also* British Nationality Act 1981, c. 61, §§ 37 & 51(2), http://www.legislation.gov.uk/ukpga/1981/61, *archived at* https://perma.cc/8KW5-XDVX.

[51] Ireland Act 1949, 12, 13 & 14 Geo. 6, c. 41, http://www.legislation.gov.uk/ukpga/Geo6/12-13-14/41, *archived at* https://perma.cc/BS3C-23T8.

[52] Representation of the People Act 1983, c. 2, § 4(1), http://www.legislation.gov.uk/ukpga/1983/2, *archived at* https://perma.cc/KUW9-PCZX.

[53] Electoral Commission, *Who is Eligible to Vote During a General Election?*, http://www.electoralcommission.org.uk/faq/voting-and-registration/who-is-eligible-to-vote-at-a-uk-general-election (last visited Dec. 23, 2015), *archived at* https://perma.cc/3VDP-HEQT.

[54] HOUSE OF COMMONS LIBRARY, DEPARTMENT OF INFORMATION SERVICES, TOTAL NUMBER OF MPS, PEERS AND STAFF, Mar. 15, 2012, Parliamentary Information List, Standard Note, SN/PC/02411, http://researchbriefings.files.parliament.uk/documents/SN02411/SN02411.pdf, *archived at* http://perma.cc/93L2-MZ4W.

[55] *Westminster Parliamentary Constituency*, OFFICE FOR NATIONAL STATISTICS, http://www.ons.gov.uk/ons/guide-method/geography/beginner-s-guide/electoral/westminster-parliamentary-constituencies/index.html (last visited Dec. 8, 2015), *archived at* http://perma.cc/TX28-BGZD.

Commissions. The Boundary Commissions recommend changes to the boundaries of the constituencies they are responsible for reviewing to ensure that each Member of Parliament represents a proportionate number of constituents who are eligible to vote.[56]

C. Registering to Vote

Provisions for the registration of voters in the UK are made through regulations under the Representation of the People Act 1983.[57] In the UK, local councils maintain voter registration lists (commonly known as the "electoral roll" or "electoral register"). The information held on the electoral roll is used for general elections, European Parliament elections, local government elections and, depending upon the persons' place of residence, elections to the National Assembly for Wales or the Scottish Parliament.[58]

Voter registration is not automatic and requires positive action (registration) on behalf of the individual wishing to vote. The electoral roll is compiled from three main sources:

- An annual canvass conducted by the Local Council between August and November. Voter registration forms are delivered to homes in the Local Councils area. Households are required by law to complete and return the form listing all their residents who are eligible to vote on October 15 of that year.[59] If the information on the form received by the household is accurate, registration can be renewed by phone or the Internet.

- Rolling registration by individual voters, who can register at any time by completing a registration form and sending it to the local electoral registration office.

- Online registration by individual voters, who can register at any time by completing and submitting an online registration form.[60]

The penalty for failing to complete the voter registration form or for providing false information is a fine of up to £1,000 (approximately US$1,500).[61] Additionally, failure to register results in the individual not being able to vote in any election, and also has a negative impact on his or her ability to obtain credit, as credit reporting agencies use the electoral roll to verify names and addresses of credit applicants.[62]

---

[56] Parliamentary Constituencies Act 1986, c. 56, sched. 2, *as amended*, http://www.legislation.gov.uk/ukpga/1986/56, *archived at* https://perma.cc/8RWM-SLDD.

[57] Representation of the People Act 1983, c. 2.

[58] *Registering to Vote*, GOV.UK, https://www.gov.uk/register-to-vote (online registration site for voting; last visited Dec. 23, 2015), *archived at* https://perma.cc/H72B-MCNH.

[59] Representation of the People Act 1983, c. 2, § 10.

[60] GOV.UK, *supra* note 58.

[61] Representation of the People (England and Wales) Regulations, 2001, SI 2001/341, ¶ 23, http://www.legislation.gov.uk/uksi/2001/341/made, *archived at* http://www.legislation.gov.uk/uksi/2001/341/made.

[62] Representation of the People (England and Wales) (Amendment) Regulations 2002, SI 2002/1871, ¶ 114, http://www.legislation.gov.uk/uksi/2002/1871/made, *archived at* https://perma.cc/DW6X-G2F4.

The electoral register can be updated on a rolling basis with additions, deletions, or amendments. Individuals who move out of the voting district can submit a new voter registration form to be listed on the electoral register in their new district. Applicants must provide their old address so that the Electoral Registration Officer of the new district can notify the old district of the move.[63]

D. Voter Turnout

There were 45,325,100 UK parliamentary voters in 2014;[64] 66.1% of the electorate voted during the general election in 2015, the highest turnout in eighteen years.[65]

E. Replacing Members of Parliament

Once elected, Members of Parliament cannot directly resign their seat.[66] The only way that a seat can be vacated is through death, disqualification, dissolution, expulsion, or elevation to the Peerage. When a parliamentary seat becomes vacant, a writ for a by-election is issued.[67] To prevent long-standing vacancies of seats, these writs are normally issued within three months of the vacancy.[68] If the vacancy occurs during a parliamentary recess, the Speaker of the House is permitted to issue a writ for election during this time.[69]

There appears to be no legislation or procedure to replace a large number of MPs. It is likely that the normal procedure for appointing MPs through by-elections would be followed in these circumstances. For example, in 1985, fifteen members of the Unionist Party vacated their seats in protest over the Anglo-Irish Agreement. As technically Members of Parliament are not permitted to reign from their seats, a legal loophole was used by these members, whereby they were appointed to an office for profit under the Crown, which disqualified them from sitting an am MP. By-elections were subsequently held to fill the vacancies.

During World War II, many seats were left vacant when MPs were involved in government services or became active members of the armed forces. The government formed a coalition in

---

[63] GOV.UK, *supra* note 58.

[64] *Electoral Statistics for UK, 2014*, OFFICE OF NATIONAL STATISTICS (Apr. 16, 2015), http://www.ons.gov.uk/ons/rel/pop-estimate/electoral-statistics-for-uk/2014/stb---2014-electoral-statistics.html, *archived at* https://perma.cc/W23P-PM28.

[65] Sarah Knapton, *General Election 2015: Highest Turnout Since Tony Blair Landslide*, TELEGRAPH (May 8, 2015), http://www.telegraph.co.uk/news/general-election-2015/11592557/General-election-2015-highest-turnout-since-Tony-Blair-landslide.html, *archived at* https://perma.cc/7X7L-9WR4.

[66] House Resolution, 2 March 1623, COMMONS JOURNAL (1547–1628) at 724; *see also* HILAIRE BARNETT, CONSTITUTIONAL AND ADMINISTRATIVE LAW (2000).

[67] The process of obtaining a writ is through a warrant from the Speaker of the House being directed to the Clerk of the Crown in Chancery. On the receipt of the Speaker's warrant, the writ is issued by the Clerk of the Crown and transmitted in pursuance of the provisions of the Representation of the People Act 1983, ch. 2. Neglect or delay in the delivery of the writ, or any other violation of the Act, is an offence; and in the event of any complaint being made the House will also inquire into the circumstances. ERSKINE MAY, *supra* note 19, at 33.

[68] Speaker's Conference on Electoral Law, 1973, Cm. 5500.

[69] Recess Elections Act 1975, c. 66, http://www.legislation.gov.uk/ukpga/1975/66, *archived at* https://perma.cc/XX5D-WPYP.

1940 and agreed upon an electoral truce, during which the parties agreed not to contest by-elections. Instead, the local constituency association of the party that had won the seat in the last election nominated a candidate.[70] However, despite this agreement, some elections were still contested when parties considered that the candidate was too radical.

V. Legislative Process

Legislative powers in England and Wales are vested in Parliament. Like the US, the legislature is bicameral. Passing an Act of Parliament requires the consent of both Houses of Parliament—the House of Lords and House of Commons—and then the Act must be given Royal Assent.[71] There are many stages that a Bill must pass through in each house of Parliament before it will receive Royal Assent and enter into law. The various stages occur in each House. The bill is first introduced and read and then debated. It then passes to the committee stage, where it is examined in depth. Once the committee stage is completed, the bill goes to the report stage and then back to be read and debated again before it is passed over to the other house, where this process occurs again.

It is a principle that the supreme authority of the Queen in Parliament is sovereign, which means that Parliament alone has the authority, with Royal Assent, to enact or repeal legislation.[72]

Some argue that this sovereignty has been eroded as Parliament no longer has exclusive legislative control over many areas now that the UK has joined the European Union (EU) and permits it to directly impose enforceable rights and obligations.[73] In addition, the courts have ruled that EU law has precedence over the national law of the UK when there are inconsistencies.[74] Despite a ruling from the House of Lords stating that it could not overturn an Act of Parliament and grant "rights directly contrary to Parliament's sovereign will,"[75] in cases where national law directly conflicts with obligations imposed by EU law, the European Court of Justice has "affirmed . . . that a national court which, in a case concerning [European] Community law, was precluded from granting interim relief by a rule of national law, must set aside that rule."[76]

Private Members' bills may also be put forward by Members of Parliament who are not Ministers. These bills are afforded significantly less time in Parliament for debate and

---

[70] TANFIELD, *supra* note 24, at 9. Tanfield states that there were seventy-five contested by-elections and sixty-six uncontested elections.

[71] Parliament Act 1911, 1 & 2 Geo. 5, c. 13, http://www.legislation.gov.uk/ukpga/Geo5/1-2/13, *archived at* https://perma.cc/F9JT-76TL.

[72] TANFIELD, *supra* note 24, at 19.

[73] 1 House of Commons, European Scrutiny Committee, The EU Bill and Parliamentary Sovereignty: Tenth Report of Session 2010–11, Dec. 7, 2010, HC 633-I, 2010–11, ¶¶ 18–19, http://www.publications.parliament.uk/pa/cm201011/cmselect/cmeuleg/633/633i.pdf, *archived at* https://perma.cc/SP5D-P6D3.

[74] Macarthys Ltd. v. Smith, [1981] 1 All E.R. 111 [120].

[75] R v. Sec'y of State for Transp., ex p Factortame, [1990] 2 A.C. 85 [142]–[143].

[76] R v. Sec'y of State for Transp., ex p Factortame, [1991] 1 A.C. 603.

discussion and, as a result, are rarely enacted, but they frequently serve to raise awareness of an issue.[77]

VI. Executive Branch

The Crown is the Head of State and has legal powers, although these are now largely ceremonial. The Crown must act upon the advice of its Ministers, who form the executive and are appointed by the Prime Minister. Ministers are typically elected Members of Parliament and thus are required to answer for their actions in Parliament. The term "Crown" often refers interchangeably to either the Monarch or executive; because the powers of the Monarch have been drastically reduced, however, the term is primarily used to refer to the executive branch of the government, which is deemed to act on the Monarch's behalf and is responsible for policy making. The actual role of the executive is not defined in legislation and, in response to a question in the House of Commons calling on the Prime Minister to define his role, Prime Minister Tony Blair noted that the Prime Minister's roles "including the exercise of powers under the royal prerogative, have evolved over many years, drawing on convention and usage, and it is not possible precisely to define them."[78]

One of the most important powers vested in the executive is the power to send forces into armed conflict. In Britain, this power rests with the Prime Minister, who may technically exercise it without formal parliamentary approval. The government has recently conducted a public consultation on its powers to go to war and has stated that it

> believes that the ability to exercise the prerogative power to deploy the armed forces without requiring any formal parliamentary agreement is an outdated state of affairs in a modern democracy. It has proposed that a detailed House of Commons resolution should set out the processes Parliament should follow in order to approve any commitment of Armed Forces into armed conflict.[79]

One major contrast with the US system of government is that the English courts can challenge the constitutionality of legislation only with regard to its compatibility with EC law. The incorporation of the European Convention on Human Rights into the national law by the Human Rights Act 1998 gave British citizens a number of directly enforceable rights.[80] However, owing to the sovereignty of Parliament—the principle that Parliament is legislatively supreme and thus there are no legal restrictions on the matters it may legislate—judges cannot strike down an Act

---

[77] *Private Members' Bills,* PARLIAMENT.UK, http://www.parliament.uk/about/how/laws/bills/private-members (last visited Jan. 6, 2016), *archived at* https://perma.cc/EMF2-WY58.

[78] HOUSE OF COMMONS SELECT COMMITTEE ON PUBLIC ADMINISTRATION, FOURTH REPORT, Mar. 4, 2004, § 43 (Lord Hurd citing Prime Minister Tony Blair, 15 Oct. 2001, Parl Deb HC (2001) col. 818W, http://www.publications.parliament.uk/pa/cm200304/cmselect/cmpubadm/422/42205.htm#note40, *archived at* https://perma.cc/VP8V-VUGX.

[79] HOUSE OF LORDS SELECT COMMITTEE ON THE CONSTITUTION, WAGING WAR: PARLIAMENT'S ROLE AND RESPONSIBILITY, 15th Report of Session 2005–6, HL235-I, ¶ 103, http://www.publications.parliament.uk/pa/ld200506/ldselect/ldconst/236/236i.pdf, *archived at* https://perma.cc/J7BR-AJE3.

[80] Human Rights Act 1998, c. 42, http://www.legislation.gov.uk/ukpga/1998/42, *archived at* https://perma.cc/V87Q-6C9B.

of Parliament if it finds it to be unconstitutional or invalid, even if they find it to be incompatible with the Human Rights Act. When the House of Lords does declare an Act to be incompatible with the Human Rights Act, the result is that Parliament must determine how to address the incompatibility.

The operation of this procedure substantially altered the relationship between the executive and judiciary, and initially caused some friction, particularly with regard to the government's robust antiterrorism legislation. In 2004 the House of Lords declared that the government's system of "preventive detention" for terrorist suspects was not compatible with the European Convention on Human Rights, resulting in a period of open hostility from members of the executive towards the judiciary, with the Secretary of State reportedly claiming they were "fed up with having to deal with a situation where Parliament debates issues and judges overturn them."[81] The Lord Chief Justice of England and Wales was allegedly referred to by a member of the executive as being a "muddled and confused old codger."[82] In a statement that demonstrates a significant difference between the role of the courts in the US and the UK, a member of the British executive claimed that "if public policy can always be overridden by individual challenge through the courts, then democracy itself is under threat." [83] The position of the principle of parliamentary sovereignty was reiterated by the executive, which stated that "it is ultimately for Parliament to decide whether and how we should amend the law."[84]

---

[81] Michael Kallenbach, *Yesterday in Parliament*, TELEGRAPH (Mar. 7, 2003), http://www.telegraph.co.uk/news/uk news/1423930/Yesterday-in-Parliament.html, *archived at* https://perma.cc/6W5N-NQTC.

[82] Francis Elliot, *Britain's Top Judge "Forced Out by Bullying Blunkett,"* INDEPENDENT (Oct. 30, 2004), http://www.independent.co.uk/news/uk/crime/britains-top-judge-forced-out-by-bullying-blunkett-7906421.html, *archived at* https://perma.cc/LP35-F5EY.

[83] Rachel Sylvester, *Blunkett Accuses Judges of Damaging Democracy*, TELEGRAPH (Feb. 21, 2003), http://www. telegraph.co.uk/news/uknews/1422661/Blunkett-accuses-judges-of-damaging-democracy.html, *archived at* https://perma.cc/C2AN-LU2E.

[84] 428 PARL DEB HC (6th ser.) (2004) col. 1589, http://www.publications.parliament.uk/pa/ld200405/ldhansrd/ vo041220/text/41220-18.htm, *archived at* https://perma.cc/WMR4-PCZF.